Canadian Criminal Law

Cover design by Pat Dacey

Canadian Criminal Law

Steven N. Spetz

Pitman Publishing

A Division of Copp Clark Limited

Vancouver   Toronto   Montreal

© Pitman Publishing 1972

PITMAN PUBLISHING
517 Wellington Street West, Toronto, Canada M5V 1G1

COPP CLARK PUBLISHING
517 Wellington Street West, Toronto, Canada M5V 1G1

SIR ISAAC PITMAN AND SONS LTD.
Pitman House, 39 Parker Street, Kingsway, London, W.C. 2
P.O. Box 6038, Portal Street, Nairobi, Kenya

SIR ISAAC PITMAN (AUST.) PTY. LTD.
Pitman House, Bouverie Street, Carlton, Victoria 3053, Australia

PITMAN PUBLISHING COMPANY S.A. LTD.
P.O. Box 9898, Johannesburg, S. Africa

PITMAN PUBLISHING CORPORATION
6 East 43rd Street, New York, N.Y. 10017 U.S.A.

ISBN 0 273 04102 9
Library of Congress Catalog Card Number: 72-80641

Pitman Publishing
517 Wellington Street West
Toronto, Ontario M5V 1G1

Printed and bound in Canada.

Upon the completion of a book such as this, it is customary to express appreciation to someone who has contributed much to make it all possible. I can only think of one person, my very wonderful wife, who excused me from doing the dishes so I could write, kept the children from ransacking my notes and breaking my typewriter, and sat up late at night correcting my several thousand spelling mistakes. To Glenda.

Contents

Introduction

Canadians know a great deal about the law. They know they may not buy alcohol until they reach a certain age. They know they may not steal. They know they may not kill anyone. They expect to be pulled over to the side if they are found driving ninety miles an hour on a city street. They know the officer will demand to see a valid driver's licence. The laws that Canadians know about would fill volumes.

Then, again, the laws that Canadians do not understand would fill volumes at least as great in size. Some of the statutes are so obsolete that probably no one has even heard of them. Some are still on the books only because they have been totally forgotten and no one is interested enough to bother having them repealed. But there are significant laws that play an everyday role in our lives, and these too are unknown to Canadians.

How effective is a law if nobody knows about it? If a person breaks a law in true ignorance, is he really guilty of an offence? The courts say yes for "Ignorance of the law is no excuse." That's fine, but how does a citizen learn about the thousands of statutes on the books, not to mention the thousands of rules set down by government regulatory agencies? We could all study the law in detail, but who has the time or the ability to understand it all? Where can the books be found, except in law libraries?

The primary responsibility for informing Canadians about the law rests with the government. It is an obvious principle that no government can keep its laws secret and demand that citizens obey what they have never heard about. This problem worried the Babylonian King Hammurapi (or Hammurabi as most texts spell it) before 2000 B.C. He knew that his courts were at a standstill because everyone, including the judges, was totally confused about the laws. Old laws had never been repealed even when new ones were passed superseding them. Hammurapi spent many years "codifying" or sorting out the many laws, casting aside old and unjust ones. He had the final code of laws carved on a large stone which was erected in front of the palace. The stone was found by archeologists in 1902, but it took many more years for language experts to decipher the writing and figure out the code.

The ancient Hebrews were very careful to teach their children the law. Moses received more than just the Ten Commandments; there are many more laws laid down in the Book of Exodus.

The Romans were proud of their ability at formalizing laws and in the height of their power they carried them throughout the Empire. But laws once neglected become unintelligible. In the sixth century A.D. the Emperor spent nearly every waking moment recodifying Roman law and he completed the task in just two years. In recognition of his work he took the title Justinian, meaning "The Just".

The Emperor Napoleon I was interested in law almost as much as he was interested in war. He prepared an elaborate and remarkable set of laws for France, which later became known as the Code Napoleon. Most French-speaking parts of the world still use the code he prepared as a basis for their laws.

In our modern society, we no longer expect the people to find out about the laws by reading stone tablets. The publicizing of law is regarded as just as important as it ever was, and it is largely achieved through the news media. The people have only to keep their eyes and ears open to learn what the law now states. And it is their responsibility to do so.

Knowing the law is a really dual responsibility. The government must make every effort to publicize. Government publications explain any changes in detail. But it is recognized that the news media provide the best means in fulfilling their normal duty of informing the public. The responsible citizen must attempt to keep himself informed. If he ignores all efforts to instruct him in the law, then he has no justification for pleading ignorance as an excuse for violating it.

Another place that more and more is being recognized as a source of information is the school classroom. It is conceivable that in the near future a course in Canadian law will be compulsory for every student.

The object of this book is to inform the reader about some aspects of Canadian criminal law. It is not all-inclusive nor is it intended to serve as a legal guide or pocket-lawyer. Hopefully it will be informative and encourage the reader to take an active interest in criminal law that will last throughout his life. I believe that with a basic understanding of criminal law and knowledge of individual rights and safeguards every Canadian can take a more meaningful part in shaping the law to keep pace with an ever-changing society.

HOW TO STUDY LAW

A law student has a real job ahead of him. Everyone tells him to work as he never worked before, and if he is the sort of individual who is determined to make good, he plunges in to storm the citadel. Suddenly, he finds he has entered a strange world. *Mens rea, actus reus, res ipsa loquitur*, and other peculiar terms peer at him in what he thought was a dead language. He sits in the library, memorizing facts and trying to fix words in his mind. Believing he has them down cold, he takes his first test and confidently writes pages which miss the boat entirely. He naturally asks, "What's wrong?" "What does the teacher want?" "What am I trying to accomplish?" "How should I study?" The problem is much the same for the ordinary citizen trying to gain a working knowledge of the law.

In a sense, laws are long lists of rules. A few lawyers have devoted a lot of time to learning all those rules. But, with ever-changing laws, this process becomes unending and rather futile, and in fact completely unnecessary for the average citizen. Instead we should realize that *law* is a word that denotes the whole process by which society provides for orderly relations among people within that society. Rather than try to *memorize* each individual rule, it is far more important to see *how* the rules are applied and to understand *how* to solve legal problems as they are actually solved in our legal system. What the student seeks is something he can use and apply.

This is why it is very useful to study actual cases where the law has been applied. It is much easier to understand a law when you see it in action. And at the same time, case law is a cornerstone in our system. Cases which have major importance are recorded and referred to by lawyers and judges alike. Every nation has produced its great judges, whether they be King Solomon or Mr. Justice Cartwright of our Supreme Court. In the opinions they gave when deciding cases, immense wisdom has been found and adopted by generations of people to come. More important, the case decision makes it clear how the judge interprets the wording of the law in view of the needs of his own day. Many laws are not clearly worded, so that in practice considerable interpretation has to be made. After you read the law, its meaning may not be particularly clear. After you read a case which illustrates that law, the meaning usually emerges much more clearly.

In reading a case, or attempting to decide one, examine first the facts that are presented. Establish in your mind just who did what, before attempting to apply the law to it. Next, work out generally what sections of the Criminal Code might apply. Perhaps only one can be employed to deal with the case. Sometimes several sections might possibly apply. Read again the sections of the law in this book which you believe are relevant to the question. Read the illustrative cases that follow the sections to amplify certain points. What you are trying to do is to find that part of the law which most properly relates to the facts, and to find other cases which were similar and which shed light on possible solutions. Do not make a snap judgement. All cases must have two sides, or there would not be any need for lawyers and judges; the outcome would be automatic. If you are writing your answer out, organize it along these lines:

General Restatement of the Facts of the Case
Write a short paragraph that repeats the most significant facts of the case. Do not copy the entire case over again, but hit only the highlights.

Arguments Which the Crown (Prosecution) Would Put Forward
Assuming that conviction is the Crown attorney's objective, what are the facts and the pertinent sections of the Criminal Code that will be the key to his case?

Arguments Which the Defence Would Put Forward
Pinpoint the facts in the case which offer a defence. Are there possible weak points in the Crown's case? Are there facts which under the wording of the Criminal Code would make conviction difficult, if not impossible? Assume that you are the accused person—how are you going to try and save yourself?

Final Conclusion
A decision must be reached, of guilty, not guilty, or in a few cases no decision because a hung jury found the case impossible to decide. Weighing both sides of the case, give your opinion as to the final outcome, and then support that opinion. Why would the jury reject the Crown's arguments? What was it in the defence's case that was convincing? This is where logic comes into play. If there is no precise answer in criminal law because the case appears unique, then derive a decision based upon principles of fairness and common sense. The important thing is not to get the "right" answer, but to demonstrate sound reasoning for the answer you deduced from the facts of the case. Students often worry that they are "wrong" and will be arguing and writing a conclusion for a guilty verdict when in the actual case the defendant was found not guilty. This is not important, although we all like to be right. Since every case is decided on its merits, there is no such thing as a right or wrong answer, only a good or poor answer.

Another important aspect of studying law is discussion. The greatest justices in history took time to consult others and seek their opinions. Judges can make mistakes, and feel genuinely reassured to know that if they do there are higher courts that can correct them. Students will obviously make mistakes and perhaps overlook the heart of a question and get bogged down in a minor point or two. Discuss cases, questions, and the very meaning of the law with other students, with teachers, or parents. Law is a living subject, which pertains to us all. Classroom discussion is significant though time sometimes prevents discussions from being long enough. Each person will learn something from others, even if it is only how confused he is!

Outside reading is very useful. Many libraries have books

which are related to law even if they are not purely law books. Novels such as *In Cold Blood* or biographies of men such as Clarence Darrow make excellent reading in enhancing your study of law. Newspapers devote considerable space to crimes, trials, and appeal proceedings. Entire articles are common in newspapers and magazines concerning unjust laws, penitentiary life, new laws and a host of other topics.

There are many more possible suggestions to put forward regarding a successful study of law, but at this point I think the student has enough to get started. The important point to remember is that it is not the study of *facts* that makes law so interesting, but rather the study of *law in action*.

The Nature of Crime

In Canada, there is one book of law that governs the criminal law for the entire nation. This is The Criminal Code of Canada. Therefore, what is an offence when committed in Quebec will also be an offence when committed in Ontario. (Note that the word *offence* is normally used instead of the word *crime*.)

This is not true in the United States. There the fifty separate states all have their own criminal laws. It is possible for something, such as gambling, to be legal in Nevada and illegal in Florida.

The Criminal Code of Canada defines, explains, and directs the enforcement of criminal law in Canada. The Code covers all the offences, explains their nature, sets maximum punishments, and dictates how the criminal proceedings must take place.

The Criminal Code does not define what a crime or offence really is. However, the traditional viewpoint which we inherit from early English common law leads us to assume that a crime is an, "intentional violation of the law as it exists, which renders a harm to society."

To constitute a crime, there must be both a *criminal act* and a *guilty mind*. Whether or not a criminal act has occurred is governed by the facts of the case and whether or not the Criminal Code prohibits the act. The question of a guilty mind is a more difficult one.

The law holds that if a person does not have the mental capacity to plan, conceive, and commit a crime, and does not understand the nature or consequences of his actions, then he cannot be guilty of a crime. This generally affects two groups: children and insane persons. About children, the Criminal Code has this to say:

12. No person shall be convicted of an offence in respect of an act or omission on his part while he was under the age of seven years.

13. No person shall be convicted of an offence in respect of an act or omission on his part while he was seven years of age or more, but under the age of fourteen years, unless he was competent to know the nature and consequences of his conduct and to appreciate that it was wrong.

The Criminal Code seems to tell us that no child under the age of seven is intelligent enough or mature enough to commit a crime. It is possible to conceive of cases where this would not be true. Those who read *The Bad Seed* or saw the movie, would conclude that a precocious child could commit a dangerous or violent act—could even kill someone. However, should such a thing occur, the Criminal Code suggests that the correct response of society would not be to imprison, but to provide mental health care to such a child. Between ages seven and fourteen, a child is normally not tried in criminal court for offences, but the Crown may try the child if there is reason to believe that the child knew the nature and consequences of his acts.

A much-publicized example of this took place in London, England in 1969. Two girls aged eleven and thirteen were charged with murdering a three-year-old boy. The Crown attempted to prove that the girls understood what murder is, that they planned and committed the murder for a thrill, and that they were fully responsible for their actions. The jury convicted the younger of the two girls, but decided the older was mentally subnormal and under the influence of the other girl. The younger girl received a life sentence.

Regarding insane persons, the Code has this to say:

16. (1) No person shall be convicted of an offence in respect of an act or omission on his part while he was insane.

(2) For the purposes of this section a person is insane when he is in a state of natural imbecility or has disease of the mind to an extent that renders him incapable of appreciating the nature and quality of an act or omission or of knowing that an act or omission is wrong.

(3) A person who has specific delusions, but is in other respects sane, shall not be acquitted on the ground of insanity unless the delusion causes him to believe in the existence of a state of things, that, if it existed, would have justified or excused his act or omission.

(4) Every one shall, until the contrary is proved, be presumed to be and to have been sane.

The Criminal Code also directs that no insane person stand trial. If the person is insane at the time of trial, even though it is believed he was sane when the offence was committed, the person shall be placed in a mental hospital until judged sane and able to stand trial. If sanity never returns, then the person will remain in an institution the remainder of his life.

A difficult question arises when the accused claims "temporary insanity". Canadian courts have been more reluctant than American courts to honour this defence. A person who commits an offence in a rage is not normally successful in pleading insanity. The two rules that must be met are that the accused was, (1) incapable of appreciating the nature and quality of his acts, and (2) did not understand that what he did was wrong.

A man who found out that his partner was stealing from the business confronted him in an angry argument. The partner admitted stealing and then accused the first man of equal wrongdoing. The man went home, got a gun, returned to the office and shot his partner. His defence of insanity was not accepted since he understood fully what he was doing and that it was wrong.

A husband found his wife and her lover in bed. He took a shotgun from another room and shot them both. The man died, the woman did not. The jury rejected the plea of insanity, but returned a verdict of manslaughter rather than murder, accepting the explanation that there was severe provocation.

Insanity was accepted as a defence in an interesting case which involved drugs. A young man on LSD killed his mother-in-law after having delusions that she was the devil and was after him. He stabbed her repeatedly while shrieking that he was slaying the devil. The jury accepted his defence that he was so deranged from the drug that he had no criminal intent but was under a delusion.

There is no simple rule regarding insanity. Each case must be decided on its own merits and the psychiatrist has become a very familiar figure in the criminal courtroom. Generally, lack of self-control, emotion, rage, and other violent states do not constitute insanity, for the person still knows that what he is doing is wrong, but does it anyway. The accused must prove to the satisfaction of the court that he was so drugged, drunk, or deranged as to be incapable of criminal intent. The court is often difficult to persuade. One rule of thumb which is often used is to consider whether or not the accused would have committed the offence if a policeman had been standing next to him. A sane man would think twice, and knowing the policeman was right there, change his mind. An insane man would not care about the presence of the policeman since he would not feel he was doing anything wrong.

If the court agrees with the accused that he was insane at the time, it does not mean he will walk away free. The court often commits the accused to a mental hospital until he is deemed well enough to return to society. For this reason, insanity is not a plea used except for very serious cases.

POINTS TO PONDER

1. Would you favour altering the age limit to some higher or lower level than fourteen as capacity to commit crime? For what reasons do you suppose it was originally placed at that age?

2. If a person committed a crime while under the age of fourteen, but did not come to trial until after his fourteenth birthday, should he be tried in criminal court?

3. What would be included under the meaning of "disease of the mind"?

4. A person acting under an irresistable impulse has been termed to be acting under "Automotism". What would this term imply and would this constitute a valid defence as insanity?

5. Under what circumstances could drunkenness be a successful defence as a form of insanity? You could start the discussion by considering this quotation taken from a recent case: "a psychopath who goes out intending to kill cannot escape the consequences by making himself drunk before doing it."

6. If a person committed an offence while genuinely suffering amnesia (loss of memory) should he later be convicted if he regained his memory but had no recollection of the offence?

Our Criminal Laws

In attempting to organize a book concerning criminal law, there are a variety of methods available. One is to try and lump items together according to their nature. Another is to commence with minor offences and progress to serious offences.

A third method is to arrange the sections of the Criminal Code alphabetically, permitting the reader to search for a topic of particular interest more quickly and also permitting the book to serve as a ready reference. This is not the way the Criminal Code is organized, but most persons who are not very familiar with the Code must rely heavily upon the subject index in the Code to find anything. By arranging sections alphabetically, I have given no offence more serious consideration than any other, although some require more explanation. The reader should be able to locate a particular topic more quickly without use of an index, a time-saving feature.

Usually, each section includes the appropriate parts of the Criminal Code and cases which illustrate how they are applied. Don't let the wording of the laws put you off. Laws look confusing because they must try to be as accurate as possible and to leave nothing open to question. (And as we discussed before, even then lawyers often argue about what a law really means.) This need for accuracy makes the sentences look very long and repetitive because of all the details that must be included. If you can't understand all the provisions of a law when you've read it, try looking at the cases that follow and then coming back to it. Often this will clear up the problem.

However, not every section is heavily illustrated with case examples. This is because some are very easy to grasp at first reading. Others require special explanation and extensive illustration to bring home key points. Not all the cases are from Canadian courts. Some are taken from courts in the United States and Great Britain. This is possible in many instances because of the similarities that exist between nations that base their criminal laws upon English common law. This is not to say that the laws are identical in all English-speaking or Commonwealth nations, but just that there are many similarities.

It will probably help if before you start you understand some terms which will often recur. For example, an offence punishable on summary conviction is a minor offence which can be dealt with quickly in the courts; an indictable offence is a serious, major crime. Students are probably familiar with American courtroom procedure through watching courtroom dramas on television, so it will be sufficient to point out that the Crown is the plaintiff in all Canadian criminal cases, and the Crown Attorney is the equivalent of the American District Attorney. Canadian court cases are referred to as *Regina v. Doe*—*Regina* means the Queen, *v.* stands for versus or against, and the name of the defendant is substituted for *Doe*. If a king is on the throne at the time of the trial, *Rex* will be used instead of *Regina*.

Other legal terms will also come up in the book, but as they will only be used a few times they will be explained as they occur.

Abortion

Intentional abortion, or the premature termination of a pregnancy, causing the loss of an unborn child, is illegal in Canada except under special circumstances. The Criminal Code states:

> 251. (1) Every one who, with intent to procure the miscarriage of a female person, whether or not she is pregnant, uses any means for the purpose of carrying out his intention is guilty of an offence and is liable to imprisonment for life.
>
> (2) Every female person who, being pregnant, with intent to procure her own miscarriage, uses any means or permits any means to be used for the purpose of carrying out her intention is guilty of an indictable offence and is liable to imprisonment for two years.

Note that the Criminal Code considers everyone guilty who has anything to do with procuring the miscarriage—not just the person who performs the abortion.

In a recent case, a young woman died from an infection which appeared following an unsuccessful abortion. Investigation later led to the trial of the abortionist, the woman's mother, and the woman's boyfriend. The mother and boyfriend were charged because they had located and paid the person who performed the abortion and were thereby guilty of procuring the miscarriage.

Selling or advertising drugs for the purpose of causing a miscarriage is similarly illegal.

Abortion is an extremely touchy subject. It involves social, moral, and religious values, as well as legal ones. Some groups, especially certain women's groups, are demanding legal abortions. They want the decision to rest solely with the mother and her doctor, not with society. To strengthen their arguments they point to the thousands of secret abortions that are performed every year by anyone from sympathetic doctors to self-styled witches. A woman who wants an abortion will obtain one, whether the law allows it or not. Illegal abortions are sometimes done with crude instruments, even with coat hangers. Women will swallow powerful drugs that sometimes kill both mother and child. Or these drugs may not bring about the miscarriage and the child may be born defective. Supporters of legal abortions want proper hospital facilities for the woman seeking an abortion so that she does not have to submit to the ministrations of a quack.

Other groups urge abortion as a means of population control. Birth control methods do not seem to be reducing the birth rate sufficiently. Abortion must help to solve the problem or we will populate ourselves right out of existence. However, most people would agree that birth control is preferable to abortion.

Another argument is that an unwanted child starts life with severe disadvantages. Psychiatrists say that children who are born unwanted will rarely be accepted by their parents. The rallying cry here is "Every child a wanted child."

On the other hand, the anti-abortion groups remind us that we must remember what abortion is—the taking of a human life. They maintain that the fact that the child is not yet born does not change its status as human life. Our criminal laws forbid the taking of another's life, and morally speaking a defenceless, unborn child needs as much protection as any living person against being killed.

Part of the argument seems to revolve around determining when life actually begins. When does a person become a human being? At birth, or at conception? Those who oppose any sort of abortion consider the foetus to be life, a human being. The Criminal Code would apply a different interpretation, as evidenced by the wording of Section 221 (1): "Every one who causes the death, in the act of birth, of any child that has not become a human being, in such a manner that, if the child were a human being, he would be guilty of murder, is guilty of an indictable offence and is liable to imprisonment for life." This definition rules out the theory that a person is a human being prior to birth, at least as far as Canadian criminal law is concerned.

Opponents to abortion add that if we permit the killing of the very young, then what will be the next step—mercy killing of the very old? Our system of law says everyone has a right to life. They feel that legalizing abortion would make a very drastic and unalterable change in that basic law. It should not be adopted without careful consideration about all the possible effects.

Recently the law has been changed to allow abortions in Canada under special conditions. These are called therapeutic abortions and may be performed in an accredited hospital under the following circumstances.

The woman's doctor must lay her case before a hospital committee for therapeutic abortion. A majority of the members must agree that abortion is necessary "because in their opinion the continuation of the pregnancy of the female person would be, or would be likely to, endanger her life, or health and have so stated in a certificate given to the medical practitioner who will perform the abortion." (The doctor who performs the abortion must not be a member of the committee.)

This does not afford much of an opening for a woman who wants an abortion simply because she is unmarried or because she does not want more children. Nor does it assist a woman who fears that the *child* will be unhealthy. The law considers only the woman's health.

Several years ago an alert woman doctor noted an increase in the birth rate of deformed babies, particularly of babies without limbs. The investigation which followed led to a German-made drug called Thalidomide which was being prescribed by doctors to relieve discomfort and tension during pregnancy. The drug was then withdrawn, but when the news reached the public, many frightened expectant mothers who had been taking the drug feared their babies would be deformed. Some sought abortion rather than take the risk. Under existing law, they could not qualify because their own health was not in danger. Some went to have abortions in other countries where the laws were different.

There are parts of the world where abortion is legal. In January 1973 the U.S. Supreme Court ruled that state laws prohibiting abortion were unconstitutional. The ruling held that the decision to have an abortion may be made by a woman and her doctor, although the state may regulate the abortion procedure. It is not unlawful for a Canadian to travel to the United States for the purpose of having an abortion.

In November 1973 a Montreal doctor was acquitted of performing an illegal abortion. The doctor's defence rested upon Section 45 of the Criminal Code which says a surgical operation is deemed a medical necessity for the benefit of the patient. At the time of writing the Crown had appealed the decision.

POINTS TO PONDER

1. If abortion were legalized, would the next step be mercy killing of the elderly and infirm? Would this be morally right or wrong? What about mercy killing of the hopelessly insane, as was done during the Nazi period in Germany?

2. Should the abortion law be liberalized to permit abortion if the child will probably be born defective? Examine this question in view of such disasters as the one caused by Thalidomide.

3. If a woman travels to New York for an abortion, does she completely escape the criminal laws of Canada?

4. If a person sold a drug to a woman which was designed and intended to cause a miscarriage, but the drug didn't work, has an offence been committed?

5. Suppose a person sold a drug that, among other uses, could cause abortion. He knew this, but asked no questions when he sold it. Has an offence been committed?

PROJECT

Conduct a survey among friends, relatives, and other acquaintances regarding this question:

Should Canada liberalize abortion laws?

Try to get a reasonable cross-section of persons by age, sex, occupation and social class. Aim for at least fifty responses. It may be more interesting to separate answers according to sex. Compile your answers along the following lines (you may think of other reasons for or against which you want to add, and those answering may have their own reasons):

RESPONSES

For Liberalized Abortion Laws		Against Liberalized Abortion Laws	
Reasons	No.	Reasons	No.
Should be private decision of mother and doctor		Abortion is as morally wrong as murder	
Abortions will be performed anyway		Abortion is unnecessary Can find someone to adopt the child	
Would help population control		There are better means available to control population	
Other: Specify		Other: Specify	

Comments

Accessory

The person who actually commits an offence may not be the only one involved and may not be the only one punished. For example, if two persons plan an offence, but only one commits it while the other waits at home, both are guilty of the offence. The law also states that if one person explains to another how to commit an offence, but does not intend or expect to share in the proceeds, he is still guilty. An example of this was the discovery of a "school for pickpockets" operating in New York City. The school trained young persons in the art of picking pockets, whether they operated alone or in groups. For the "final examination" a department store mannequin was fully dressed as a well-to-do man. The candidate had to pick all his pockets without breaking thin threads attached to the dummy's clothes. Breaking a thread meant careless work and failure. The school did not share in the proceeds of their graduates' crimes, but made its income by charging the students set fees to learn the trade. The school and its instructors were prosecuted for "counselling and procuring others to commit an offence." Another term for this is accessory before the fact.

Having seen that everyone involved in planning an offence is considered guilty of the offence, we must also examine the part others may play after an offence has been committed. Such a person is called an accessory after the fact. The Criminal Code states:

23. (1) An accessory after the fact to an offence is one who, knowing that a person has been a party to the offence, receives, comforts or assists him for the purpose of enabling him to escape.

(2) No married person whose spouse has been a party to an offence is an accessory after the fact to that offence by receiving, comforting or assisting the spouse for the purpose of enabling the spouse to escape.

(3) No married woman whose husband has been a party to an offence is an accessory after the fact to that offence by receiving, comforting or assisting in his presence and by his authority any other person who has been a party to that offence for the purpose of enabling her husband or that other person to escape.

Generally, we can see that anyone who knows that a person has committed an offence must refrain from rendering any help whatsoever that aids the offender to escape. This prohibits such things as providing food, shelter, money, transportation, or refusing to tell the police of the whereabouts of the offender. Friendship or family ties do not excuse someone for aiding an offender.

A group of men went into a bar. One of them was notorious for being rude and troublesome when drunk. The other men knew this. True to form, the man started an argument with a waiter. The bar owner then ordered all the men to leave. The man jumped up, struck the bar owner, and then started a fight with the waiter. He knocked the waiter down and kicked him several times. His friends succeeded in containing him, and dragged him out of the bar. All of them being somewhat more sober now, they got in their car and drove off. Later they were arrested, and all were charged. The chief offender was charged with assault causing bodily harm. The other men were charged with being accessories after the fact. Their plea that they were justified in removing their friend was not accepted. They had assisted someone to escape knowing that an offence had been committed.

The significant lesson here is that one should choose friends wisely. The assistant warden of a penitentiary told me that many convicts would not be in prison today if they had the sense to avoid pals bound for trouble. If a person hangs around with individuals prone to commit illegal acts, it will just be a matter of time until he is implicated either by being a party to the offence, or an accessory after the fact.

As mentioned earlier, family ties are not considered a valid excuse for helping an offender.

A man shielded his son after a robbery. The police inquired if the father knew where the son was. They told him his son was suspected of an offence. The father denied knowledge, and by doing so became an accessory. Two nights later, the father put food in the car and hid his son in the trunk. He drove to another town and rented a cottage. A week later, he bought a used car and gave it to his son, wishing him luck in eluding the police. The son was caught, but not until after a shoot-out with police. Investigation revealed the father's part in the attempted escape, and he was convicted as an accessory after the fact.

Only one family tie is considered sufficiently strong to excuse a person for helping a fugitive. This is the relationship of marriage. A man or woman cannot be prosecuted for assisting in the escape of his or her spouse. A wife who shields her husband, provides him money, or transports him to another place to escape, cannot be charged as an accessory. However, she must not commit or take part in another offence while doing so. For example, if a wife is helping her husband escape one offence, and he tells her to drive the car while he robs a gas station to get more money, she will be prosecuted for the robbery with her husband. Helping him escape is one thing—helping him commit more crimes is another.

Also, a woman cannot be charged as an accessory for helping someone escape with her husband. If two men commit a robbery and flee to the home of one man, the wife's efforts to help her husband and the other man escape together are justified. Were this not so, the law would hold that while she could help her husband, helping the other man was an offence. Realistically, we must assume that the two fugitives plan to stay together, and that the wife cannot help her husband and not the other man at the same time.

A question is sometimes raised concerning a person's duty to report offences. Does a person who fails to report to the police an offence that he knows was committed, commit an offence himself?

The answer is no. The Criminal Code does not contain a specific order that all crimes must be reported by persons having knowledge of them. The victim of a crime doesn't even have to report it if he doesn't want to. Without a complaint, there will be no prosecution. The law assumes that citizens mindful of their duty will want to curb crime and will voluntarily report offences they know about. Anyone who has reason to believe that an offence has been committed may report the information to a magistrate but he does not have to do so if he does not want to. On the other hand, falsely reporting an offence which you know did not take place is an offence punishable by five years in prison.

POINTS TO PONDER

1. A wife is never charged as an accessory for assisting her husband escape. Why is this same protection not extended to parents whose natural instinct is to protect their child? Should the law be amended to permit this?

2. Refer a moment to the discussion of abortion. Suppose a woman went to the apartment of a friend and said, "I need a place to stay for a while. I've had an abortion and I'm very sick." If the friend takes her in, and generally looks after her, discuss the legal position of the friend as an accessory.

3. If a husband arranged an abortion for his wife, would he be immune from punishment as an accessory? Could he be charged for something else?

Alcohol Offences

The federal government does not dictate to the provinces controls over the consumption of alcohol. Hence, the Criminal Code has little to say about the matter of consumption. In the past, the legal drinking age has been twenty-one but in many provinces the age has already or will soon be lowered to eighteen. Whatever the age limit, possession of alcohol by anyone under that age is a provincial offence, and providing alcohol for someone under age is also an offence. An interesting exception is Manitoba, where recent legislation allows parents to offer beer or wine to their children not only at home but also in licensed restaurants.

The laws concerning liquor in Ontario are found in the Liquor Control Act, and subsequent regulations are issued by the Liquor Control Board.

However, the problem of drunkenness as distinct from controls on the sale and consumption of alcohol is one that the Criminal Code does discuss. Being drunk is not an offence in itself. If a man quietly goes to a bar, gets totally stoned, and returns home in a cab, he commits no offence. And drinking in one's own home, even to excess, is regarded as a personal privilege.

There are circumstances, though, that make just being drunk an offence. For example, a person who is constantly drunk in the same home as a child, even if it is his own home, is said to corrupt the child. This is prohibited by the Criminal Code:

168. (1) Every one who, in the home of a child, participates in adultery or sexual immorality or indulges in habitual drunkenness or any other form of vice, and thereby endangers the morals of the child or renders the home an unfit place for the child to be in, is guilty of an indictable offence and is liable to imprisonment for two years.

The friendly drunk described above who goes home quietly is a wise man. His friends might not be so quiet and thereby run afoul of the law:

171. Every one who

(a) not being in a dwelling house causes a disturbance in or near a public place,

(i) by fighting, screaming, shouting, swearing, singing or using insulting or obscene language,

(ii) by being drunk, or

(iii) by molesting other persons; . . .

is guilty of an offence punishable on summary conviction.

Our man was also wise to take a cab home—wiser than his friend who might try to drive his own car home. The law takes a dim view of those who drive under the influence of alcohol or of drugs that impair judgement. Such drivers kill and maim thousands of persons every year and cause millions of dollars of property damage.

234. Every one who, while his ability to drive a motor vehicle is impaired by alcohol or a drug, drives a motor vehicle or has the care and control of a motor vehicle, whether it is in motion or not, is guilty of an indictable offence or an offence punishable on summary conviction and is liable:

(a) for a first offence, to a fine of not more than five hundred dollars and not less than fifty dollars or to imprisonment for three months or to both:

(b) for a second offence, to imprisonment for not more than three months and not less than fourteen days, and

(c) for each subsequent offence, to imprisonment for not more than one year and not less than three months.

Note that the drunk doesn't have to actually be *driving*, he just has to have care or control of a motor vehicle.

A policeman found a drunk in a parking lot trying to start his car by inserting his house key in the ignition. The officer arrested the man for impaired driving—even though he hadn't

managed to start the car. Being in the driver's seat was enough
to assume he had care and control of the motor vehicle.

Another case involved a drunk who went off the road into a
field. The investigating officer found him behind the wheel,
sleeping it off, the car resting firmly on its roof! This also
constituted impaired driving, even though the car wasn't sitting
on its wheels. If the driver is in the motor vehicle for the
purpose of setting it in motion, or has previously set it in
motion, this constitutes impaired driving. In another case a
drunk found sleeping in the back seat of a car was held not to
be guilty of impaired driving.

A recent amendment to the Criminal Code has aroused much
public controversy. It involves a test for impaired driving. If
requested to do so by a police officer, a driver must provide a
breath sample. The breath sample is fed into a machine that
measures the amount of alcohol present. If the sample shows an
excess of 80 milligrams of alcohol per 100 millilitres of blood,
the driver is guilty of an offence punishable by a fine not less
than $50 and not more than $1,000 or to imprisonment for not
more than six months, or both.

The thing that upset Canadians most was that this new law
did not permit the driver to refuse to take the test. In fact,
refusal to take the test could mean a penalty just as severe as
the one above. Several cases went to the Supreme Court of
Canada contesting that no one can be forced to take such a test,
any more than he can be forced to take a lie-detector test, for
the test is self-incrimination, or being forced to testify against
yourself. The Supreme Court upheld the law and we must all
live with it. Canadians can take some comfort from knowing
that similar laws in other countries are more severe. In
Germany, for example, the law permits the police to compel a
driver to go immediately with them to a hospital and have a
sample of his blood taken and tested to make an exact
measurement of the proportion of alcohol in the blood. If the
test indicates impaired driving, a jail sentence is *automatically*
imposed. So we should count our blessings, and law or no law,

for the good of everyone, drink a little less and drive a little more carefully.

In 1973 the Supreme Court of Canada ruled that a motorist has the right to consult his lawyer before agreeing to take a breath test, unless it appears that the motorist is only trying to delay the test. The test must be administered within two hours after apprehension by the police. Any attempt to delay the test longer than that will result in conviction for refusal to take the test.

To turn to other points, it is not an offence to make certain alcoholic beverages in Canada. Beer and wine, which are produced by natural fermentation, can be made in the home. Amateur wine-making is becoming a popular pastime in Canada, today. Some of the wine-making firms are even giving classes to enthusiasts to foster the love of wine among more people. However, these amateur vintners are prohibited from selling their products, since a licence is required to do so. And at the same time, it is illegal to distill alcohol in the home. This is not the same process as natural fermentation; it requires a distilling apparatus commonly known as a "still." Owning or operating a still is a serious offence, so the moonshiner hides his stills carefully.

In Ontario, one offence which young people may commit is being a "found-in." A found-in is a person present in a residence where liquor is being consumed and a person under age is also present. The under-age person need not be drinking, just the fact that he is present is illegal. If four persons were drinking at a cottage, and the police investigated and found that one of the four was not of legal drinking age, all could be charged with being found-in.

POINTS TO PONDER

1. Alcoholism has been termed a sickness, not a crime. One man was arrested and convicted forty-eight times in eleven years for various offences committed because of alcohol addiction. Do you think chronic alcoholics should be treated as criminals or as sick persons?

2. Would you favour more severe penalties for impaired driving? What would be possible alternatives? The permanent loss of a driver's licence? An automatic jail sentence?

3. The age limit for legal drinking has been lowered from twenty-one to eighteen years in most provinces. Was this a wise move? As a class project, survey the local police department and Crown attorney and inquire if arrests or violations have notably increased.

4. See if your local police department will demonstrate the use of a breathalyzer.

Arson

Setting fire to something may have a legitimate purpose. Fire cooks food, eliminates waste and provides heat. It is one of our oldest and most useful tools.

Setting fire may have other motives. A pyromaniac gets a thrill from setting fires and watching all the excitement of the fire department and police, crowds, etc. Unless he is caught, he may kill people and cause fantastic property damage.

Fires are also deliberately set for other reasons: for vengeance, to collect on fire insurance, or just to remove something unwanted in a hurry. Setting a fire illegally is called *arson*, and the Criminal Code has this to say:

389. (1) Every one who wilfully sets fire to

(a) a building or structure, whether completed or not,

(b) a stack of vegetable produce or of mineral or vegetable fuel,

(c) a mine,

(d) a well of combustible substance,

(e) a vessel or aircraft, whether completed or not,

(f) timber or materials placed in a shipyard for building, repairing or fitting out a ship,

(g) military or public stores or munitions of war,

(h) a crop, whether standing or cut down, or

(i) any wood, forest, or natural growth, or any lumber, timber, log, float, boom, dam or slide,

is guilty of an indictable offence and is liable to imprisonment for fourteen years.

(2) Every one who wilfully and for a fraudulent purpose sets fire to personal property not mentioned in subsection (1) is guilty of an indictable offence and is liable to imprisonment for five years.

Two men had an argument with a motel owner about noise. When the owner ordered them to leave, the men left behind a device rigged by placing a lighted cigarette inside a book of matches, on top of some papers. When the cigarette burned down, it ignited the match heads and the papers caught fire. The two men were far away when the blaze was actually discovered, but an alert fire investigation team was able to reconstruct what had taken place. They were both imprisoned for arson.

A small store owner was in severe financial trouble. He was overstocked with merchandise, sales were down, and creditors were closing in. He had ample fire insurance, so one night he burned his business down to collect on it and save himself from bankruptcy. Fire investigators determined that the blaze was set with gasoline and the owner was prosecuted for arson.

A man had an old tool shed on his property. He had no use for it as the wood was too rotten. To tear it down would be hard work and the material would have to be carried away. He decided to eliminate it the easy way, he set fire to it. A neighbour called the fire department. The fire chief asked how the blaze started and the man told him he started it. He was angry that the fire department had meddled and put out the fire. When arrested for arson, the man was indignant. It was his shed, he contended, and he could do what he wanted with it. Legally his contention was false, and he was fined and warned not to use arson as a method of getting rid of unwanted buildings in the future.

Another important issue in cases of fire is negligence. If a building is required by local ordinances to have fire extinguishers and other fire-fighting devices, but they are not there, a fire which results in destruction or loss of life may bring a severe penalty to the owner—up to five years in prison.

Unfortunately, many people feel that they can use fire for whatever means they wish, such as burning off weeds or destroying an unsightly building. They run the risk of arrest for arson. Before starting a fire, you should check with the fire inspector or fire department in your locality to determine if it is lawful to do so.

POINTS TO PONDER

1. Do you think a five-year prison term is sufficient penalty for arson?

2. Should a person who carelessly starts a fire, by smoking in bed for example, be charged with some form of arson? Note the word "wilful" in the section.

3. Should a person be punished for failing to turn in a fire alarm even if he didn't set the fire? (Turning in a false alarm is an offence.)

Assault

There are many degrees of assault, depending upon the intent of the person causing it and the results inflicted. Assault may be committed on its own or in conjunction with another offence, such as robbery or causing a disturbance. The Criminal Code states:

244. A person commits an assault when, without the consent of another person or with consent, where it is obtained by fraud,

(a) he applies force intentionally to the person of the other, directly or indirectly, or

(b) he attempts or threatens, by an act or gesture, to apply force to the person of the other, if he has or causes the other to believe upon reasonable grounds that he has present ability to effect his purpose.

Note from paragraph (b) that the mere threat by word or gesture of doing bodily harm is grounds for conviction of assault, provided there is reasonable grounds to believe the assault could be carried out.

A very small man started a fight with a very large man at a neighbourhood bar. The small man, about 90 pounds soaking wet after six beers, threatened to "thrash the @!†+" out of the larger man. The other man, a two-hundred-pound steel worker, was annoyed by this nonsense and complained to the manager. Since the smaller man had no real capability to thrash the larger man, there was no assault, since there was no reasonable grounds to believe he could carry out his threat, and the larger man did not believe a word of it. If the larger man had been threatening the smaller man, it would have been a case of assault since he could certainly carry out the threat.*

Assume that the smaller man is evicted from the bar for annoying the patrons. If he returned later with a gun and threatened to "shoot that big @!†+*" the matter is entirely different. Size, strength, or stature have no relevance when a weapon is involved. A gun is sometimes called an "equalizer" meaning that a small man equalizes his chances with a larger man by holding a gun. However if there is only one gun, there is nothing equal about it—the man with the gun has all *the advantage. There is a very real question of assault here, since the small man certainly has the ability to carry out what he threatens to do.*

Common assault is punishable by up to six months in prison. If common assault causes injury to the other person, a two-year prison sentence may be given. If a gun or other weapon is used and it causes bodily injury (wounding), the maximum sentence is fourteen years in prison. This is true even if the gun goes off accidentally.

The law denies citizens the right to threaten or jeopardize the safety of another person, or intentionally to do injury to another person. This prohibition includes actions such as throwing acid or rocks, or even spitting on someone.

A situation may arise when a threat of assault is made not directly to a person, but indirectly. For example, a man hears from others that another man is planning to cause him bodily harm or damage his property in some way. The threat has not been made directly, but just communicated to him in a roundabout manner to let him worry about it. What should the intended victim do, just wait until the assault takes place? Go and have it out with the other man first?

A little-known section of the Criminal Code provides ample protection in such a case.

745. (1) Any person who fears that another person will cause personal injury to him or his wife or child or will damage his property may lay an information before a justice.

(2) A justice who receives an information under subsection (1) shall cause the parties to appear before him or before a summary conviction court having jurisdiction in the same territorial division.

(3) The justice or the summary conviction court before which the parties appear may, if satisfied by the evidence adduced that the informant has reasonable grounds for his fears,

(a) order that the defendant enter into a recognizance, with or without sureties, to keep the peace and be of good behaviour for any period that does not exceed twelve months, or

(b) commit the defendant to prison for a term not exceeding twelve months if he fails or refuses to enter into the recognizance. . . .

746. A person bound by recognizance under section 745 who commits a breach of recognizance is guilty of an offence punishable on summary conviction.

Robert Wilks testified against Howard Grasser at his trial for robbery. Grasser went to prison for five years. When the term was nearly up, Wilks learned that Grasser told a visitor to the prison that the first thing he was going to do after his release was "TO GET WILKS!"

The week before his release, Grasser was brought into court and ordered to observe the peace towards Wilks. He agreed to do so, but two weeks after release he appeared at Wilks' home brandishing a rifle. Grasser was returned to prison to serve a six-month sentence.

No citizen needs to fear for his personal safety or for his property. If such a situation should arise, do not hesitate to seek protection from the police and the court.

POINTS TO PONDER

1. Hunters periodically shoot other hunters because carelessness leads them to mistake persons for animals. Should charges
of assault be laid against them? Would the fact that "It was an
accident," excuse the shooting?

2. Sometimes a person is not accused of assault on the grounds
that he had "undue provocation." How much provocation
should be allowed before excusing a person for assaulting
another? How is provocation to be measured? See the section
on manslaughter.

3. Would squirting someone with a hose be assault? If the person committing the act thinks it is a prank, but the victim does
not, how will it be decided whether it is assault or not?

Assembly

The right of assembly, that is the coming together of people to exchange ideas, to hold religious or political meetings, or to meet for other lawful purposes, is a very old and very important right. Civil wars and revolutions have been sparked when authorities ordered persons to stop assembling or prohibited any public meetings. The Canadian Bill of Rights recognizes the right of all Canadians to *the freedom of assembly and association*.

Does this freedom mean there may be no restrictions at all regarding assembly and association? It does not. A convict on parole may be required to avoid association with any known ex-convict or any person with whom he associated prior to getting into trouble. Breaking this rule can result in the revocation of the parole and a return to prison. A mob blocking traffic in order to protest something does not have the protection of the Bill of Rights. Like anything else, freedom is not absolute, it must be responsibly exercised and lawfully carried out with due regard for the rights of others. The Criminal Code states what constitutes unlawful assembly:

64. (1) An unlawful assembly is an assembly of three or more persons who, with intent to carry out any common purpose, assemble in such a manner or so conduct themselves when they are assembled as to cause persons in the neighbourhood of the assembly to fear, on reasonable grounds, that they

(a) will disturb the peace tumultuously, or

(b) will by that assembly needlessly and without reasonable cause provoke other persons to disturb the peace tumultuously.

(2) Persons who are lawfully assembled may become an unlawful assembly if they conduct themselves with a common purpose in a manner that would have made the assembly unlawful if they had assembled in that manner for that purpose.

(3) Persons are not unlawfully assembled by reason only that they are assembled to protect the dwelling house of any one of them against persons who are threatening to break and enter it for the purpose of committing an indictable offence therein.

67. Everyone who is a member of an unlawful assembly is guilty of an offence punishable on summary conviction.

"Disturbing the peace" is a rather ambiguous phrase. It is not carefully defined and each case must be examined on its own merits. Generally, we assume that the "peace" is a state of affairs under which quiet, calm, and orderly citizens can go about their business without interruption, annoyance, undue noise, fear from disorderly conduct, or harrassment.

To illustrate subsection (1) let us assume that a group of motorcyclists gather at a shopping centre. They begin roaring around the parking lot, making shoppers fear that they or their cars may be struck. The group also attracts a large audience of young people who watch this unusual behaviour. The store owners call the police because of (a) the disturbance already created, and (b) fear that it will worsen. The police order everyone to disperse and go about their lawful business, warning that this is an unlawful assembly.

To illustrate subsection (2) let us assume that a group of strikers picket a plant. Their strike and picketing are lawful and orderly. Then the strikers learn that the company plans to bring in other men to take their jobs. The word spreads that the company is going to use these non-union "scabs", and a large number of workers gather at the plant entrance. As cars try to enter, they are blocked, rocked, threatened, and even damaged. Rocks are thrown at the windows and tires are slashed. The previously lawful assembly has now become an unlawful one.

An event which recently has become popular is the rock festival which brings together thousands of persons in a field or other suitable place to listen to continuous music for several days. Opponents of these events complain about noise, unsanitary conditions, property damage, additional police costs, and the illegal use of drugs. This has led many communities to ban such festivals. Promoters are now fighting such bans in the courts, claiming the right to freedom of assembly. They point out that if someone like Billy Graham wanted to hold a huge religious rally, this would be permitted. Coming together peacefully to listen to music is similarly guaranteed under the Bill of Rights. The results of these court battles will make interesting reading.

An unlawful assembly may progress into a full riot. If twelve or more persons are involved, a peace officer may command silence and proclaim that a riot is in existence and order all present to disperse within thirty minutes and depart peacefully to their homes. The maximum penalty for riot is life imprisonment. An example of the proclamation of a state of riot was given at the fair grounds in Picton, Ontario, after three nights of fighting among youth groups.

POINTS TO PONDER

1. "Sit-ins" have grown in popularity as a form of protest. Do they constitute unlawful assembly?

2. Police often discourage young people from hanging around stores, etc. Are these young people necessarily unlawfully assembled?

3. Why do municipalities require groups to get permits before having parades?

Automobile Offences

If you were to line up a knife, gun, a bottle of poison, and an automobile and ask, "Which weapon is most often used to commit a crime?" the automobile should win. Some people might not understand that, but the automobile is a dangerous machine and it can be a weapon. More serious offences are committed with it than with any other. Driven by a careful, sensible driver, the car is a useful tool. Driven by anyone less than that, it kills, maims, destroys and threatens thousands of people every year, and drivers are sent to jail by the hundreds.

The conduct of motor vehicles on the highway is governed by each province. The speed limits, driver-testing, licence plates for the car, mechanical safety requirements, insurance—these matters come under provincial, not federal, laws. In Ontario the most significant items are covered by The Motor Vehicle Act and The Highway Traffic Act.

The federal law *does* come into the picture when the automobile is misused. As discussed in the section on alcohol offences driving while under the influence of alcohol or drugs is a serious offence. Refusal to provide a breath sample for analysis is severely punished.

The offence of criminal negligence or dangerous driving is even more severely punished. The Criminal Code states:

233. (1) Every one who is criminally negligent in the operation of a motor vehicle is guilty of

(a) an indictable offence and is liable to imprisonment for five years, or

(b) an offence punishable on summary conviction.

(2) Every one who, having the care, charge or control of a vehicle that is involved in an accident with a person, vehicle or cattle in charge of a person, with intent to escape civil or criminal liability fails to stop his vehicle, give his name and address and, where any person has been injured, offer assistance, is guilty of

(a) an indictable offence and is liable to imprisonment for two years, or

(b) an offence punishable on summary conviction.

(3) In proceedings under subsection (2), evidence that an accused failed to stop his vehicle, offer assistance where any person has been injured and give his name and address is, in the absence of any evidence to the contrary, proof of an intent to escape civil and criminal liability.

(4) Every one who drives a motor vehicle on a street, road, highway or other public place in a manner that is dangerous to the public, having regard to all the circumstances including the nature, condition and use of such place and the amount of traffic that at the time is or might be reasonably expected to be on such place, is guilty of

(a) an. indictable offence and is liable to imprisonment for two years, or

(b) an offence punishable on summary conviction.

Note that subsection (2) concerns the offence which most people refer to as "hit and run". This is certainly a foolish act. Leaving the scene of an accident is practically speaking an admission of guilt, even though the driver may not necessarily be at fault.

A man struck and injured a boy riding a bicycle on a lonely road. The boy was almost entirely responsible, as he was riding the bike contrary to all the rules of the road and bicycle safety. For some reason the man panicked and drove off. The police tracked him down through a repair garage and he received a six-month suspended sentence, and later was successfully sued for damages by the boy's parents. His lawyer told him that his offence was not striking the boy, but leaving the scene and failing to render assistance. Had he stayed at the accident, he probably would have been in no trouble either criminally or in a civil law suit. Hitting the boy was not his fault, but failing to stop jeopardized his rights.

Read again the wording of subsection (1) and subsection (4). There is a certain similarity, but they are not the same. The first mentions "criminal negligence". Everyone is criminally negligent who in doing anything, or in omitting to do anything, that it is his duty to do, shows wanton and reckless disregard for the lives or safety of other persons. "Duty" here means a duty imposed by law, not a moral duty. (This is discussed more fully in the section on criminal negligence.)

The heart of this definition is "wanton and reckless disregard for the lives and safety of others". Although this sounds simple enough, it is not an easy matter to prove. Speeding, racing, showing off—while being poor driving habits and illegal, do not necessarily constitute criminal negligence. Poor driving habits or bad judgement may cause a serious accident, yet criminal negligence still cannot necessarily be proved. A driver who passes blindly on a curve is risking an accident, but he is not necessarily disregarding the safety of others. He might be very frightened for his own safety and that of others—but passes anyway, taking the calculated risk that nothing is coming the other way. To prove criminal negligence the Crown must show that the driver was aware that he was risking the lives and safety of others and was completely unconcerned about them. The driver taking a risk is perhaps quite worried about what might happen if he is wrong, and may even be working out in his mind how he will avert trouble by taking to the ditch, etc. The driver who pulls out at the wrong time because he isn't paying enough attention is not aware that others are in jeopardy, so cannot be wantonly disregarding their safety. What does constitute criminal negligence? An example of a criminally negligent driver is one who tears along a road, passes cars on both left and right, passes on hills and curves, drives at a fantastic speed, has several close calls, but does not change his method of driving at all. Here, the facts show that he is now aware that he is jeopardizing others, but by continuing his actions he shows wanton disregard for their safety. One careless act or mistake does not demonstrate criminal negligence. A continuing series of such acts may demonstrate it.

Because criminal negligence is not easy to prove, drivers are more often charged under subsection (4) rather than subsection (1). This is "dangerous driving" and is less stringent and easier to prove. Many things a driver does could be called dangerous. Excessive speeding, racing, carelessness, falling asleep at the wheel, have all been held as sufficient cause for a dangerous driving conviction. In many respects, it is a catch-all. It is worded so generally that any incorrect action behind the wheel could lead to a conviction. It also serves as a "lesser offence" for subsection (1). This means that if the Crown cannot get a conviction under subsection (1), it often will settle for a lesser offence conviction under subsection (4).

A motor vehicle which was on the wrong side of the road struck another head-on. One death occurred. The grand jury brought in an indictment for criminal negligence, since the evidence showed that fast driving was mostly at fault. The case went to the petit jury with the accused pleading not guilty to the charge of criminal negligence, but voluntarily pleading guilty to a charge of dangerous driving, a lesser offence. The jury accepted and agreed with this plea and brought in a verdict of guilty to the charge of dangerous driving.

The importance of this lies in the possible punishment. Criminal negligence is a very serious matter when a death has occurred. The maximum penalty is life imprisonment. If injury occurred, the penalty can be up to ten years imprisonment. In the case above, the defence lawyer was wisely having his client plead guilty to an offence that bears only a penalty of a possible two-year prison term. He hoped the jury would accept this guilty plea and ignore the Crown's case for criminal negligence. He was successful, and his client, who faced a possible life sentence if found guilty of criminal negligence, received a suspended six-month sentence.

Note also that if a driver has had his licence revoked or suspended, he can receive a penalty of a maximum of two years imprisonment for driving without a licence.

There are various lesser offences under provincial law. Most are explained in *The Driver's Handbook* which is available from your local police department. Even though you may have had your driver's licence for a long time, pick up a *Handbook* and review the laws. You may be surprised at how much you have forgotten . . . or never knew.

POINTS TO PONDER

1. Should the age required for driving be raised from sixteen to a higher age? Examine this from the viewpoint of emotional, physical and mental readiness to drive.

2. Would it be wise to require drivers to take another driving test, say every five years? What would such a test hope to achieve?

3. Should those convicted of dangerous driving or criminal negligence with a motor vehicle permanently lose the right to drive? If this penalty were known, would it act as a deterrent to all drivers not to drive dangerously or when impaired?

Bawdy-houses

The word *bawdy* isn't used much any more, so it is conceivable that many readers may not understand what it means. A bawdy-house, defined in the Criminal Code, is a place "that is kept or occupied or resorted to by one or more persons for the purpose of prostitution or the practice of acts of indecency."

Now the reader might say, "Oh, that kind of place." If you wonder why words such as bawdy are used, it is just a nicety. Most court officials would object if the charge was printed and worded as "running a whore house."

In many parts of the world, prostitution exists on a large scale. Some governments have given up attempts to eliminate it, and instead license it. Under a licensing system, health authorities maintain inspection procedures in the established brothels in order to prevent the spread of venereal disease.

Canadian law is not prepared to sanction prostitution in this way. The traditional Christian doctrine is that prostitution should be condemned and this is the attitude expressed in the Criminal Code of Canada. The prostitute is punished on summary conviction. More serious penalties await a person who attempts to organize prostitution. The Criminal Code states:

193. (1) Everyone who keeps a common bawdy-house is guilty of an indictable offence and is liable to imprisonment for two years.

(2) Every one who

(a) is an inmate of a common bawdy-house

(b) is found without lawful excuse in a common bawdy-house, or

(c) as owner, landlord, lessor, tenant, occupier, agent or otherwise having charge or control of any place, knowingly permits the place or any part thereof to be let or used for the purposes of a common bawdy-house,

is guilty of an offence punishable on summary conviction.

The wording indicates that just about everyone in a bawdy-house is in trouble of some sort, even the customers. As well as this, any person who attempts to procure a female person for the purpose of aiding, abetting or compelling her to enter a bawdy-house as an inmate or to engage in or carry on prostitution may be punished by a sentence of ten years imprisonment.

Not many convictions are obtained any more under this section. There are various reasons for this. Lawmakers tend to feel more and more that it is not their business to legislate on the moral behaviour of citizens. Police departments are busy with other matters and find that because of changing attitudes conviction under this section is very difficult. If they do win a conviction, the penalty is often no more than a fine which the accused can easily afford to pay. Society as a whole is less shocked by such acts than it was when the law was formulated. Movies such as *Irma La Douce*, which stars an actress playing the role of a prostitute, are now considered quite acceptable.

Whether prostitution is evil or not, it should be noted that investigations in both Canada and the United States have concluded that organized prostitution provides money which the underworld uses to finance other criminal activities.

POINTS TO PONDER

1. Should all restrictions on prostitution be removed from the Criminal Code so that it becomes a matter of individual choice?

2. Some European countries have taken to licensing houses of prostitution and requiring medical checks to prevent the spread of venereal disease. Why has Canada not adopted such an approach?

Betting and Gambling

For some people, gambling is a disease. Others make their living by it. Every conceivable device has been used to encourage people to bet on the outcome of almost any event. Many people in North America find betting on horse races and dog races very exciting. In South America cock fights hold a similar attraction. Prize fighters such as Mohammed Ali receive from promoters advance promises of more than one million dollars per championship fight. In these events, the winner is supposedly the contestant with the most skill and it takes skill to pick the winner. In other types of gambling, only chance or luck is at stake. Drawing a number out of a hat offers no scope for the skill of the player.

Racetracks in small towns, bingos in church basements, and raffles on street corners give clear evidence that some forms of gambling are at least winked at by the authorities. Not all gambling is. In this section, we shall try to distinguish between legal and illegal forms.

LEGAL GAMBLING

Private bets and wagers

If two friends make a friendly bet between themselves on the outcome of a football game, this is perfectly legal. It is a private bet and is not something which injures society. However, if the loser refuses to pay, the court will not assist the winner in collecting.

Permitted Lotteries

The Government of Canada and the provincial governments may license or conduct their own lottery scheme. Also, a charitable organization may hold a lottery if it first acquires a licence from its local municipality. Each province may set the limits of the prizes. Ontario has set a maximum of $3,500 for all the prizes totalled together in the same lottery. This gives ample room to sell lottery or raffle tickets on large items such as automobiles. In addition, permission may be obtained by special licence for larger lotteries.

Licensed Racetracks
Pari-mutuel betting at a racetrack licensed by the provincial government is lawful within the limits set by the government as to how many races may be held in a single day, etc. All other "bookie" places are illegal. The Supreme Court of Canada recently held that a downtown business that takes bets to the track for betters is not illegal, as long as the downtown office is not itself making the bet with the customer.

ILLEGAL GAMBLING

Lotteries
A lottery is a method of determining a winner just by random selection. The Irish Sweepstakes is a well-known international lottery. More locally, "pools" are formed to bet on sporting events, or even on the stock market. These lotteries and pools are illegal: conducting them is an indictable offence punishable by two years imprisonment. Their popularity makes them no less illegal, although arrests are few.

Three-card Monte
This game involves three playing cards, one usually a queen. The queen is placed in the middle, all cards turned face down. The operator then moves the cards around quickly, using sleight-of-hand to lose the card with the others. A member of the audience must then pick out which card is the queen. To double the bet, he can try to name the position of all the cards. Because of the endless ways the operator can cheat, such as marking the cards, or using a confederate planted in the audience, this is considered by most prudent persons a true sucker game.

Table Games
A gambling casino contains many games played on tables using

wheels, dice, cards, machines, and other devices. There are too many different games to name them all. Some countries permit casinos, such as the elegant ones in Monte Carlo and Las Vegas. Canada permits no gambling casinos. Everyone who keeps a betting or gaming house may be punished on summary conviction. And whether it is a dice game or a poker game with some friends, none of these games can legally be played in Canada— as a means of gambling. If they are played for fun, not for money, no offence is committed. Games of chance for money are sometimes permitted by special licence at agriculture fairs, exhibitions, etc.

Slot Machines
The "one-armed bandit" is illegal in all forms in Canada. This device is a slot machine with rotating wheels with pictures on them, such as oranges, cherries, and so on. The three wheels revolve independently, and if by chance the same pictures come up together, a pay-off of three for one, five for one, ten for one, or "jackpot" occurs. You drop coins in at the top, pull the handle, the wheels turn, and you either win or lose, depending upon what comes up. The chief problem with such machines is that they can be tampered with very easily never to pay off, or to pay off so seldom that profits to the owner are fantastic. Some machines have been rigged so that some of the coins dropped in are stolen and when a jackpot is hit, only part of the coins inside drop out to the winner.

The law is not trying to snuff out church bingo games raising money for a useful purpose. It does intend to discourage organized gambling run on a large scale by underworld criminals. Organized crime gets a great deal of easy revenue from encouraging gambling. A convicted mobster, Joseph Theresa, told a US Senate Committee in 1971 that "Crime all starts with gambling—and ends with gambling. Without gambling, organized crime would be nowhere." Governments have slowly realized that prohibiting all gambling was a mistake. It forced people who wanted to play a game of chance to sneak or deal with criminals. It provided lucrative profits for organized crime. Making gambling illegal did not stop people from wanting to do it.

Recent moves in legislation have been aimed at providing some outlets for the gambling instinct and doing some good at the same time. Objectives now are:

To legalize certain forms of popular gambling to permit those who want to play to do so without breaking the law

To permit charities to run lotteries, raffles, and bingos for worthwhile purposes

To force the criminals out of business by having government-run race tracks and betting

Some might call this a retreat from a principle, joining the other side because you couldn't lick them. Perhaps, but without the retreat illegal gambling would still persist. Of course, it will anyway but hopefully on a smaller scale. And law-abiding persons can play bingo, bet on a horse or buy a raffle ticket without breaking the law. At the same time, profits from gambling will go into the treasuries of charities and governments rather than into the pockets of criminals.

POINTS TO PONDER

1. Some forms of gambling are legal, others are not. Why not make all forms legal? For example, if bingo lovers can have their game, why can't Chinese Fan-Tan players enjoy theirs legally?

2. Which games do you consider to be pure luck and which involve skill? Compare bingo to poker.

Bigamy

Polygamy, or having more than one spouse at the same time, is still practised in certain parts of the world. Canada, because of its Christian heritage, does not accept this principle and permits only one spouse at a time to any person. (This may be a blessing in disguise since two spouses would mean two sets of in-laws!)

Bigamy is committed when a marriage takes place in which the bride or groom is already married. The Criminal Code states:

> 254. (1) Every one commits bigamy who
>
> (a) in Canada,
>
> (i) being married, goes through a form of marriage with another person,
>
> (ii) knowing that another person is married, goes through a form of marriage with that person, or
>
> (iii) on the same day or simultaneously, goes through a form of marriage with more than one person; or
>
> (b) being a Canadian citizen resident in Canada leaves Canada with intent to do anything mentioned in subparagraphs (i) to (iii) of paragraph (a) and, pursuant thereto, does outside of Canada anything mentioned in those subparagraphs in circumstances mentioned therein. . . .
>
> 225. (1) Every one who commits bigamy is guilty of an indictable offence and is liable to imprisonment for five years.

From this the reader should note that not only can the already-married person be prosecuted, but also the person he or she marries if that person *knew* bigamy was being committed by the marriage. Leaving Canada does not afford protection if the parties return to Canada.

The matter of a previous divorce is often cited in cases of bigamy before the courts. Theoretically, a person cannot claim he committed bigamy accidentally simply because he thought he was divorced. The fact is that if the person completes the questions on the application for a marriage licence truthfully, he will disclose the previous marriage and divorce. If the divorce is not in order or recognized in Canada, the marriage licence will not be granted.

Divorces obtained in a foreign country are the most suspect. They are often not recognized as lawful in Canada because of the ease with which they are obtained. For example, at Reno, Nevada, a near automatic procedure is run. Mexican divorces have been obtained by mail. The refusal of Canada to accept these divorces is understandable.

Any person having doubts about the validity of his divorce can obtain a ruling from the Provincial Secretary in the province in which he resides.

John Fredericks and his wife wanted a divorce. They heard that the waiting time in Canada was too long, so Mrs. Fredericks went to Reno and got a divorce from her husband in two days. Later, John applied for a marriage licence to marry Glenda Sanders. Their application was turned down because the divorce was obtained in Nevada. John and Glenda went to Maryland and were married there. If they returned to Canada, John and Glenda faced prosecution for bigamy.

This does not mean that all foreign divorces are not recognized in Canada. If an American citizen married and was divorced in New York under New York laws, this would be recognized if he later moved to Canada. However, when it appears that a Canadian has gone to a foreign country solely to obtain an easy divorce, it is seldom recognized in Canada.

It is not considered bigamy for a person to remarry if he or she believes his or her spouse to be dead and this later proves to be incorrect. A person who has been missing for seven years can be legally declared dead, and the spouse may marry again without fear of prosecution for bigamy if the first spouse should reappear.

Bigamy cases seldom occur, but when they do they receive large news coverage. For some reason, many readers find these cases amusing. They are seldom amusing for the persons involved. Sordid rackets have been run involving marriage and bigamy. One man married a wealthy woman then asked her for a large sum of money. He claimed that his first wife, whom he never divorced, had turned up and demanded money to keep quiet.

The law does not prohibit two persons from living together as man and wife, even though they are not married to each other. "Common law" arrangements, as they are called, are legal; therefore, there appears to be no valid reason for a person to commit bigamy except to deceive the other person for personal profit.

POINTS TO PONDER

1. Certain nations of the world permit bigamy. Until recently, the Mormon church permitted and urged it. What is basically wrong with the practice?

2. Suppose that the birth rate of females is greater than that of males. Is it conceivable that in time, there will not be enough males and bigamy will become necessary?

Breaking and Entering

The burglar is a very real person. People who have been burglarized never forget it. Those who have not been burglarized are usually too lax until they are.

If premises are left open, the fact that a person walks in is not necessarily an offence, even though he may have no legitimate reason to be there. Of course, if he steals something, he can be convicted of theft. A drunk found sleeping in the unlocked basement of a church was not deemed to have entered for the purpose of committing an offence. A man found in the unlocked basement of a store was convicted because he could give no valid reason for his presence.

Few people go out and fail to lock doors and windows. But these devices are not a complete defence against someone who is prepared to break locks, jimmy doors, remove hinges, or cut glass or screen. For this type of entry, certain tools are needed, such as crowbars, screwdrivers, glass cutters, hammers, knives, etc. The law considers these items to be housebreaking tools, and possession of them is an offence punishable by 14 years imprisonment. This does not mean possession of a screwdriver is illegal. But when a man with a large screwdriver was apprehended at the rear of a store at about 2 a.m., and he could not give an adequate explanation of his presence he was convicted for possession of housebreaking tools. Note that as the law now stands, no break-in need actually have occurred, if under the circumstances the possession of the tools appears to be for no other purpose than breaking in. Two men caught on the roof of a building with a skylight were convicted for possession when it was deemed that the tools they had could be used to break open the skylight and enter the building. A proposed change in the Criminal Code will require the Crown to prove that the tools were intended to be used for burglary, and not merely in a person's possession.

Back to our basic offence, breaking and entering; the Criminal Code states:

306. (1) Every one who

(a) breaks and enters a place with intent to commit an indictable offence therein;

(b) breaks and enters a place and commits an indictable offence therein; or

(c) breaks out of a place after

(i) committing an indictable offence therein, or

(ii) entering the place with intent to commit an indictable offence therein,

is guilty of an indictable offence and is liable

(d) to imprisonment for life, if the offence is committed in relation to a dwelling house, or

(e) to imprisonment for fourteen years, if the offence is committed in relation to a place other than a dwelling house.

(2) For the purposes of proceedings under this section, evidence that an accused

(a) broke and entered a place is, in the absence of any evidence to the contrary, proof that he broke and entered with intent to commit an indictable offence, or

(b) broke out of a place is, in the absence of any evidence to the contrary, proof that he broke out after

(i) committing an indictable offence therein, or

(ii) entering with intent to commit an indictable offence therein.

The penalties for this offence might seem terribly severe to someone who breaks and enters a gas station and steals $14. The penalty is severe. Legal authorities will tell you that this has been a tradition in our lawmaking, to be severe with the thief who breaks and enters, particularly if he enters a home. Traditionally, the lawmakers were landed gentry, who had considerable property. They had an intense hatred of anyone who violated their property, particularly their homes. Their view of the home was that it should be the safest and most secure place in the world, and that if anyone violated it the punishment should be severe.

Judges seldom award the maximum penalty for breaking and entering, but the possibility of a severe sentence is always there.

To protect your property from breaking and entering, here are some simple rules to follow:

Have all doors mounted so that hinges cannot be removed from the outside. Hasps should also be mounted so that they cannot be removed from the outside with a screwdriver.

Have good quality locks installed. Have a chain lock on the inside to permit the door to be opened slightly to see who is outside.

Keep close control of all keys. Don't lend them to anyone.

Have window locks and catches in good working order.

Keep the garage locked. Garage tools may assist burglars to enter the house.

When going out for the evening, leave several lights on and the radio or television playing.

When away for a long period of time, stop all deliveries of mail, milk, and newspaper. Arrange for a neighbour to check your house periodically. If gone a very long time, arrange to have the grounds cared for. Tall grass indicates an absent owner.

Do not keep excessive valuables in the house.

POINTS TO PONDER

1. Is the penalty for breaking and entering too severe? With the large increase in break-ins, does a stiff maximum penalty seem to act as a deterrent at all?

2. Is it logical to charge a person for breaking *out* of a place?

3. Should stores get the same protection as homes in the severity of the penalty?

4. With the number of break-ins on the rise, is it foreseeable that the Criminal Code will be relaxed to allow some forms of man traps? See the section on man traps.

5. Many police chiefs attribute the increase in break-ins and thefts to drug abuse. Addicts take to burglary to get goods to support their drug habit. Do you accept this theory?

Capital Punishment

The term capital punishment means punishment by death—the maximum penalty for crime. The arguments over capital punishment go back a long time. Those who favour the death penalty believe it is just punishment for vile crimes and will deter others from committing the same acts. Opponents to the death penalty argue that it has never been proven to deter a single criminal from an offence and that death is unduly harsh—a life sentence would suffice.

Different countries use different methods of execution. The French only recently abandoned their famed guillotine which the inventor, Dr. Guillotine, claimed was entirely painless. In Spain, death is caused by slow strangulation inflicted by a "garrote" noose around the neck which is slowly tightened. In the United States various means are used in different states: the gas chamber, the electric chair, and hanging. Canada has always used hanging.

Those who oppose capital punishment won a victory in 1967 when an act was passed that abolished capital punishment for a trial five-year period. In 1973, the partial ban on hanging was continued for another four years.

There is an exception to the abolition of capital punishment. When the act was proposed, it was pointed out that while criminals had formerly been reluctant to shoot at policemen, because they knew a "cop-killer" was sure to hang, now with only the possibility of a life sentence, they would be less disinclined to shoot police. This jeopardized police more than ever. Also, a convict already serving a life sentence might kill a prison guard whom he disliked, figuring that since he was already serving life, he had nothing to lose.

These arguments carried strong weight, and the Criminal Code left in a provision for capital punishment in certain cases:

214. (1) Murder is capital murder or non-capital murder.

(2) Murder is capital murder, in respect of any person, where such person by his own act caused or assisted in causing the death of

(a) a police officer, police constable, constable, sheriff, deputy sheriff, sheriff's officer or other person employed for the preservation and maintenance of the public peace, acting in the course of his duties, or

(b) a warden, deputy warden, instructor, keeper, gaoler, guard or other officer or permanent employee of a prison, acting in the course of his duties,

or counselled or procured another person to do any act causing or assisting in causing the death.

(3) All murder other than capital murder is non-capital murder.

It might seem unjust that if a person murdered you, he would only receive a maximum life sentence. If he murdered a policeman, he would hang. Does this mean that the policeman's life is worth more than yours? Or if he murdered a policeman who was off-duty at the time, should he escape hanging? Whatever your feelings, the entire matter will be rehashed in 1977 and public discussion will again be very intense. However, no one has been hanged in Canada since 1962, because the federal cabinet has commuted all death sentences to life imprisonment. This is an indication that society has become increasingly reluctant to administer this very final sentence.

POINTS TO PONDER

1. Would you favour a return to capital punishment?

2. Should a more humane and painless method of carrying out capital punishment than hanging be used?

3. Does capital punishment violate the basic human right of a person, the right to life?

PROJECT

Conduct a survey among friends, relatives, and other acquaintances regarding this question:

Should Canada re-institute capital punishment (the death penalty)?

Compile your answers along the following lines. Try to get a reasonable cross-section of persons by age, sex, occupation, and social class. Aim for at least fifty responses.

RESPONSES

For Capital Punishment		Against Capital Punishment	
Reasons	*No.*	*Reasons*	*No.*
As deterrent to others		Wrong to take anyone's life	
Necessary to protect society		Does not deter others	
A just punishment		Life imprisonment suffices	
Other: Specify		Other: Specify	

Comments

Conspiracy

Conspiracy usually conjures to the mind thoughts of persons lurking around foreign capitals arranging overthrows or coups. To conspire means to plan secretly together. The plan, if it has an unlawful purpose, is illegal and all conspirators equally guilty. Generally, the Criminal Code states:

432. (2) Every one who conspires with any one

(a) to effect an unlawful purpose, or

(b) to effect a lawful purpose by unlawful means,

is guilty of an indictable offence and is liable to imprisonment for two years.

Different conspiracies have different penalties. Very briefly, they are:

Conspiracy	Penalty
To commit murder	Fourteen years
To bring false prosecution	Five to ten years
To induce a woman to adultery	Two years
To restrain trade	Two years
To commit treason	Life imprisonment (death)
To commit sedition	Fourteen years

When we speak of conspiracy we must assume the conspirators had a real and true intent to carry out their aims. If the conspiracy is only a joke, idle talk, or empty threats, the conspiracy is not real.

During the FLQ Crisis in Quebec many persons arrested were charged with conspiracy to overthrow the governments of Quebec and Canada. One defendant was so charged because he had written a notebook full of his ideas of how the revolution should be carried out and what the new government should be like. He was found not guilty. The court held that his writings were only the work of a dreamer who wanted perfection rather than a revolution. There was no real evidence that he conspired to commit an offence.

POINTS TO PONDER

1. Should conspiracy be a crime if the person does not make an active attempt to carry out his plan? Explain your answer.

2. What is sedition?

3. It has been said that, "Conspiracy exists only in men's minds." If so, how can a person be convicted for what he is thinking?

Contempt of Court

There are various ways a person may run afoul of our courts. He may misbehave, insult, or annoy the court, or he may not even show up! Contempt of court is a term which describes a variety of things. One judge said about contempt, "It is hard to define, but easy to recognize." It can best be defined as "an act of disobedience or disrespect toward a judicial or legislative body of government or interference with its orderly processes."

If you examine the Criminal Code of Canada for exact explanations, there aren't very many. The only really detailed section deals with a person who has been required to come to court by subpoena but fails to appear.

636. (1) A person who, being required by law to attend or remain in attendance for the purpose of giving evidence, fails, without lawful excuse, to attend or remain in attendance accordingly is guilty of contempt of court.

(2) A court, judge, justice or magistrate may deal summarily with a person who is guilty of contempt of court under this section and that person is liable to a fine of one hundred dollars or to imprisonment for ninety days or to both, and may be ordered to pay the costs that are incident to the service of any process under this Part and to his detention, if any.

That's what the law says—you can be jailed and required to pay the cost of being there, too.

If a person is present at a preliminary hearing of any type and refuses to be sworn or refuses to give testimony when called upon to do so, he may be sentenced to eight days in jail. If he still refuses, he may be returned to jail for another eight days, and so on. Continual refusal could mean permanent imprisonment.

In an American case, a nun was told by a boy that he committed an offence. She was later called upon to testify at his trial, but refused to do so, claiming the same "privileged information" status that priests hold. (A priest is usually not made to divulge what he heard at a confessional.) The Court did not agree that nuns have the same status as priests and sentenced the nun to eight days in jail. At the end of the eight days, she still refused to testify, and was returned to jail for eight more days. At the time of writing, she is still in jail.

Privileged information is also a right granted to lawyers who represent a client. They cannot be required to divulge conversations they had with their clients concerning the matter under litigation. If this were not so, then a defence lawyer would be the worst witness against his own client, since he would have to tell everything the accused person told him. This privilege of course does not apply if the lawyer is himself participating in an illegal act.

Canada does not have the same protection afforded by the United States Fifth Amendment. The familiar statement: "I refuse to testify on the grounds that I may incriminate myself," has no legal basis in Canada. The Canada Evidence Act does say that the written record of his testimony cannot be used against him. The police can, however, act upon the evidence to obtain further evidence.

THE HISTORY OF CONTEMPT

Setting the Criminal Code aside for a moment, we are certainly not finished with the subject of contempt. Where do other methods and manners of committing contempt originate if not in the Code? The answer lies in our legal system, which is based on English common law. Common law has its basis upon the customs and traditions of the English-speaking peoples. What is the traditional treatment of contempt?

Originally, all decisions and orders came directly from the king, who could legally "do no wrong". A citizen who failed to obey the king's laws was punished for his disrespect towards the king as much as for not obeying the law. It was his improper attitude towards his monarch that earned him his greatest punishment. Later, early courts were considered to be agents of the king, and refusal to obey their orders was considered another form of contempt for the king, and for the king's authority. Parliament was similarly regarded as the king's servant, and contempt of Parliament was recognized early as an unacceptable practice.

From this early beginning, the question of what was contempt grew until it became an offence to commit any act which showed disrespect or interfered with the judicial process. Contempt can take place in or out of court, before or after a trial, in criminal or civil proceedings—a vast area!

CONTEMPT IN THE COURTROOM

The following actions have been held as contempt during Canadian court proceedings.

Insulting protests against the judgements of the court.
Assault in or near a courtroom.
Threatening witnesses or jurors.
Blaspheming or shouting at the judge.
Insulting the judge or the authority of the court.
Resistance to orders of the court.
Interrupting the proceedings of the court.
Disorderly conduct or demonstrations in the courtroom.
Refusal to rise when the judge enters or leaves.
Foul or abusive language.
Argumentative attitude by a witness or lawyer, exceeding what is acceptable during court debates.
Applauding a verdict or jury.
Refusal to leave the court when ordered to do so.
Refusal to answer a question when ordered to do so.

Paul Rose, convicted of the murder of Labour Minister Pierre Laporte, was sentenced to thirty-eight months in prison on nineteen separate counts for contempt due to his behaviour as a witness in the armed robbery trial of Claude Morency. Sixteen citations involved refusing to answer questions put to him.

Note that lawyers are also subject to contempt citation for courtroom behaviour.

A lawyer was fined $2,000 for contempt when he asked that a Supreme Court of Canada Justice disqualify himself from hearing a case. While the Justice was out of the room, the other Justices asked to hear the reasons why the lawyer made this request. Finding his reasons to be trivial, they angrily fined him for interfering with the judicial process of the court and wasting their time.

Attorneys representing Charles Manson during his murder trial in California were sentenced to three days in jail for violating the judge's order that no newspapers be brought into the courtroom during the trial.

CONTEMPT OUT OF THE COURTROOM

Prior to a trial, certain actions may be held to be contempt because they interfere with the judicial process.

For example, a man is arrested for murder. While he is awaiting trial, a newspaper runs a full story of the crime and gives details about the man's life, including all his previous convictions. Because the prospective jurors have all read the story, they are prejudiced against the accused man. The newspaper may be held in contempt.

The general rule is that no opinionated articles are to be written until after the trial. No results of a preliminary hearing may be published without the consent of the magistrate before the trial.

Also, publications that insult, scandalize, or libel courts or judges are contempt. Refusal to obey a court order is similarly contempt.

THE PENALTY

Contempt can be dealt with by fines or imprisonment or both. There is no set limit on the penalty for most offences, but traditional sentences have indicated that it should not be unduly severe. Appeals against sentences for contempt citations are allowed and are usually successful if the judge overdoes the penalty. Contempt is normally considered a summary offence.

The question of the legality of contempt citations seems to be firmly established in our system. There is certainly room for argument that it denies freedom of speech because judges cannot be criticized as other public servants can be. If a judge reaches a poor verdict or is too lenient, and a newspaper criticizes that verdict and suggests the judge is unfit for office, can a contempt citation be brought? Usually not, unless the wording is such that it is offensive and attacks the dignity and authority of the court.

Contempt of court remains a somewhat peculiar and strange weapon that compels an attitude of courtesy and compliance with the law and court rulings. In our modern society, perhaps it is a good idea to have one place where calm, order, courtesy and quiet still prevail.

POINTS TO PONDER

1. Should a person be allowed the right to refuse to testify in a case if he has personal convictions which tell him not to?

2. Should Canada adopt something similar to the Fifth Amendment in the United States?

Counterfeiting

Counterfeit money is defined as, "A false coin or false paper money that resembles or is apparently intended to resemble or pass for a current coin or current paper money."

The penalty for making counterfeit money is imprisonment for fourteen years.

The laws regarding counterfeiting are very involved. Our discussion here will be related only to the most significant sections. Counterfeiting itself is becoming more common and more difficult to detect. Modern developments in photography enable counterfeiters to produce better quality counterfeit bills in a shorter period of time. While the counterfeiter of the 1930's might spend years engraving a printing plate, his cousin in the 1960's and 1970's is using colour photographic processes to make near perfect copies which the average citizen cannot recognize. At Expo '67 it was estimated that $50,000 to $100,000 a day in counterfeit bills were passed by organized gangs.

Other offences relating to currency include:

Clipping Coins
This is a method of cutting small amounts of silver from coins, thus gathering a small stack of silver which can later be melted down. If this is done to enough coins, a large amount of valuable silver can be stolen. Coins have the milled edge to make it harder to clip them without being detected. This trick is becoming less common since coins have very little silver in them any more. Clipping coins is punishable by imprisonment for fourteen years.

Defacing Coins
Anyone who defaces a current coin can be punished on summary conviction.

Using Slugs

Anyone who uses a washer or other slug in a meter or vending machine is guilty of an offence punishable on summary conviction.

Printing of Likeness of Notes

Anyone who reproduces the likeness of paper money in circulars, advertising, handbills, etc., is guilty of an offence punishable on summary conviction. "Pictures" of money are permissible as long as the colour, design and size are different from Canadian currency. Also producing "play money" such as is used in games like Monopoly is legal as long as it is not made to resemble money.

Minting Coins

Generally it is unlawful for anyone except the government of Canada to mint coins for commercial use of any kind. Periodically however, private mints produce collectors' coins which are intended to commemorate an event or honour famous people. An example is a series portraying the heads of the prime ministers of Canada. These coins must (1) be of a different size and thickness from genuine coins so they can not be used in vending machines, (2) bear no face resemblance to real coins, and (3) contain no precious metals.

Anyone who has received a counterfeit coin or bill must surrender it to the police. He will not be reimbursed for his loss by the government, but under no conditions should he attempt to pass it off on someone else. Even if he did not make the counterfeit bill or coin, if he knowingly tries to stick someone else with it, he commits an offence.

POINTS TO PONDER

1. What harm does counterfeiting do to society?

2. If a person made false coins that were supposedly several hundred years old and no longer current, would this be counterfeiting? If the reason he made them was to convince coin collectors they were real and get a good price for them, what charge could be brought? (See Forgery).

Credit Obtained by False Pretences

In our modern world of credit cards, charge accounts, and finance contracts, there inevitably exists a segment of society and business which has exhausted its credit by the over-use or abuse of credit. Credit bureaus help keep tabs on those who are bad credit risks. Many people criticize credit bureaus as invasion of privacy, but there is no doubt that they are here to stay and will probably expand their activities several times over during the next decade.

Credit is normally obtained by filling out some type of application form on which the applicant states his earnings and the amount he owes to others. A business which is seeking a large loan must present similar facts, in more detail, including a Balance Sheet and a Statement of Revenue and Expenses.

Now a person may be afraid that if he puts all the true facts down on his application, he may be denied credit. He is probably aware that such a decision will be based on the fact that he either pays debts late or not at all. He may be tempted to "forget" a few things and to hope the credit bureau isn't very alert that day. A business which is in financial trouble and needs a loan to avoid bankruptcy, may be tempted to produce financial statements which have been altered to make the business look much more solid than it really is. Do these persons commit an offence, or are these attempts to get credit this way just part of the game between debtor and creditor to see which is the sharper?

Since large amounts of money may be involved, the law does not view obtaining credit by deceit as a game. The Criminal Code states:

320. (1) Every one commits an offence who

(a) by a false pretence, whether directly or through the medium of a contract obtained by a false pretence, obtains anything in respect of which the offence of theft may be committed or causes it to be delivered to another person;

(b) obtains credit by a false pretence or by fraud;

(c) knowingly makes or causes to be made, directly or indirectly, a false statement in writing with intent that it should be relied upon, with respect to the financial condition or means or ability to pay of himself or any person, firm or corporation that he is interested in or that he acts for, for the purpose of procuring, in any form whatsoever, whether for his benefit or the benefit of that person, firm or corporation,

(i)   the delivery of personal property,
(ii) the payment of money,
(iii) the making of a loan,
(iv) the extension of credit,
(v)   the discount of an account receivable, or
(vi) the making, accepting, discounting or endorsing of a bill of exchange, cheque, draft, or promissory note; or

(d) knowing that a false statement in writing has been made with respect to the financial condition or means or ability to pay of himself or another person, firm or corporation that he is interested in or that he acts for, procures upon the faith of that statement, whether for his benefit or for the benefit of that person, firm or corporation, anything mentioned in subparagraphs (i) to (vi) of paragraph (c),

(2) Every one who commits an offence under paragraph (a) of subsection (1) is guilty of an indictable offence and is liable

(a) to imprisonment for ten years, where the property obtained is a testamentary instrument or where the value of what is obtained exceeds two hundred dollars; or

(b) to imprisonment for two years, where the value of what is obtained does not exceed two hundred dollars.

(3) Every one who commits an offence under paragraph (b), (c) or (d) of subsection (1) is guilty of an indictable offence and is liable to imprisonment for ten years.

(4) Where, in proceedings under paragraph (a) of subsection (1), it is shown that anything was obtained by the accused by means of a cheque that, when presented for payment within a reasonable time, was dishonoured on the ground that no funds or insufficient funds were on deposit to the credit of the accused in the bank or other institution on which the cheque was drawn, it shall be presumed to have been obtained by a false pretence, unless the court is satisfied by evidence that when the accused issued the cheque he had reasonable grounds to

believe that it would be honoured if presented for payment within a reasonable time after it was issued.

(5) In this section, "cheque" includes, in addition to its ordinary meaning, a bill of exchange drawn upon any institution that makes it a business practice to honour bills of exchange or any particular kind thereof drawn upon it by depositors.

Note that this section takes particular aim at persons writing bad cheques. Anyone writing a cheque not covered by sufficient funds must prove that he did not intentionally write a bad cheque, that he thought he had funds to pay for it. If the wording were not this way, it would be the burden of the Crown to prove that the writer intentionally wrote a cheque knowing full well there were no funds behind it. This would make conviction difficult since the writer could just claim he made a bookkeeping error or that it was just accident.

Amazingly enough, many people flirt with possible conviction under this section. They write cheques without any regard as to what their present bank balance is. They also file applications for credit and make deliberate false statements about debts, and so forth in the hope of obtaining credit by fooling the lender. Such practices are not only unethical but also can lead to criminal prosecution.

POINTS TO PONDER

1. Do you think the penalty for this offence is appropriate?

2. With the increase in credit bureaus, can we not discontinue prosecution for this offence since we have enough information to check on nearly everyone?

3. Read again subsection 320(4). Does the wording imply that overdrawing an account constitutes an offence?

4. If you accept payment in the form of a cheque and it bounces, what action is open to you?

Cruelty to Animals

There are various reasons why persons react cruelly to animals. Sometimes a person may feel that a certain animal is a pest, or he may take unlawful steps to injure an animal because it belongs to someone he dislikes. One particularly vulnerable and valuable animal is the cow. In the past if neighbours were feuding, frequently one might attack the other by destroying his livelihood—his cattle. Because of the seriousness of such acts, the penalty was and is quite severe. Anyone who kills, maims, or poisons cattle or water the cattle may drink, is subject to five years imprisonment.

Injury to other animals, such as pets, is punishable upon summary conviction. Such cases sometimes arise from a dislike one person takes towards another's pet. The pet may be trespassing or otherwise causing a nuisance and the offended person finally takes drastic action against the animal instead of legal action against the owner.

The Criminal Code does not permit mistreatment of animals, nor does it permit neglect of them. The following may all lead to summary conviction:

Staging fights between animals such as dogs or cocks.
Giving poisons or harmful drugs to domestic animals or birds.
Wilfully inflicting unnecessary suffering or pain on animals.
By wilful neglect, causing injury to animals while they are being transported.
Keeping an animal in captivity without shelter, food, or water.

A man was raising dogs to sell to medical centers for research. He collected strays and accepted give-aways whenever possible. When investigators acted upon a complaint, they found the dogs without food or water and penned together so closely they could not exercise. Some of the animals had died from malnutrition. The man was convicted and sentenced to six months imprisonment.

In nearly every community, there are animal shelters. Unwanted pets should be taken there; they are rarely refused. In this regard, owners have a responsibility to insure that pets do not have unwanted litters.

Not all acts against animals are considered cruelty. A person can protect his person, family and property against animals. Farmers may shoot animals, particularly stray dogs, that endanger their herds. Pests, such as weasels, who invade hen houses, may be trapped. Hunting during season is lawful. Animals may be used for medical research.

We can generally conclude that the law allows animals to enjoy a certain amount of protection from man. While man preys upon animals as a form of food, it is agreed that this does not permit him to inflict undue pain or suffering regardless of how the animal is to be used. For example, the controversial St. Lawrence seal hunt now has inspectors to insure that seals are killed quickly. Hunters who are careless are ordered off the ice by government supervisors. The possibility of the extermination of different species may lead to more protection in the future for many animals.

POINTS TO PONDER

1. Should a person convicted of cruelty to animals be prohibited from ever owning an animal again?

2. Does medical research upon animals constitute cruelty to animals? Under what conditions is it permitted, and who maintains safeguards against abuse?

Defamatory Libel

Libel is generally thought of as a civil matter. If a publication puts false allegations into a report or article, the injured person may sue the publication for the damage done to his reputation. Libel suits are often quite expensive. In a civil law suit, the publisher can successfully defend his case by proving that the article was true. Hence, printing the truth cannot be wrong by the standards of civil law.

There is an exception to this principle. The motive for printing the story must be a legitimate one; there must be a reason for the public to know the information. If a story is printed solely as scandal or deliberately to destroy a person's reputation, it is an offence, *whether the story is true or not.* The Criminal Code states:

262. (1) A defamatory libel is matter published, without lawful justification or excuse, that is likely to injure the reputation of any person by exposing him to hatred, contempt or ridicule, or that is designed to insult the person of or concerning whom it is published.

(2) A defamatory libel may be expressed directly or by insinuation or irony

(a) in words legibly marked upon any substance, or

(b) by any object signifying a defamatory libel otherwise than by words.

Subsection (2) paragraph (b) includes such things as large photos, drawings, statues, cartoons—any object that ridicules the person.

Note the words "lawful justification" in subsection (1). Each case must be decided upon its own merits. The following examples will help to illustrate this.

A man appointed to the post of City Treasurer in a small city was relatively unknown, although he appeared to have excellent qualifications for the job. Some investigation by reporters uncovered that he had recently moved from another province where he had been dismissed from a similar job for misuse of public funds. The newspaper ran a story exposing this and called for the man's dismissal. This story was deemed justifiable because the public had a legitimate need to know the truth.

A mayor in a city was running for re-election. His first term of office had been marked by a continuous quarrel with some council members over the police department. The mayor and the police chief wanted tough law enforcement. Some citizens felt their attitude was too tough. A group campaigning against the mayor placed an advertisement in the local newspaper showing a photograph of Adolph Hitler and Hermann Goering. The real faces had been cut away and photos of the mayor and police chief were pasted in their place. The result was a photo of the mayor and the police chief in Nazi uniforms. The caption read: "Do we need four more years of them?" Both the newspaper editor and the political group were convicted of defamatory libel.

The penalty for defamatory libel that is *known to be false* is five years imprisonment. Other defamatory libel is punishable by two years imprisonment.

In all defences against the charge of defamatory libel, it must be shown that the publication was for the public good.

POINTS TO PONDER

1. What tests could be used to establish whether a news story was in the public interest, or just printed for sensationalism?

2. Suppose a publisher prints a story obtained by one of his reporters without knowing that it was false. When he later learns it was false he retracts it. Is he guilty of defamatory libel?

Drug Offences

"Legalize pot" has become the rallying cry of those who object to the provisions of the Narcotic Control Act.

The scope of the problems involved in the control of drugs was considered too extensive for the Criminal Code, so a new and separate statute (the Narcotic Control Act) was passed in 1961. This Act sets up a schedule of substances, both natural and artificial, which are declared narcotics. Possession or trafficking these narcotics without lawful authority (such as a medical prescription) or purpose is illegal.

The schedule is quite long, but the general narcotic groups are:

1. Opium Poppy (*Papaver somniferum*) its preparations, derivatives, alkaloids and salts, including:
(1) Opium
(2) Codeine (Methylmorphine),
(3) Morphine,
(4) Thebaine,
and their preparations, derivatives and salts,

2. Coca (*Erythroxylon*) including:
(1) Coca leaves
(2) Cocaine
(3) Eogonine (3-hydroxy-2-tropane carboxylic acid)

3. *Cannabis sativa, . . .* including:
(1) Cannabis resin,
(2) Cannabis marihuana, . . .

4. Phenylpiperidines . . .

5. Phenazepines . . .

6. Amidones . . .

7. Methadols . . .

8. Phenalkoxams . . .

9. Thiambutenes . . .

10. Moramides . . .

11. Morphinans . . .

12. Benzazocives . . .

13. Apromides . . .

14. Benzimidazoles . . .

POSSESSION OF NARCOTICS

The penalty for possession of narcotics on a summary conviction for a first offence, is a fine of one thousand dollars or imprisonment for six months, or both. For a subsequent offence, the penalty is a fine of two thousand dollars or imprisonment for one year or both fine and imprisonment. Upon conviction on indictment the penalty is imprisonment for seven years.

TRAFFICKING IN NARCOTICS

Trafficking in narcotics means to manufacture, sell, give, administer, transport, send, deliver or distribute, or offer to do any of these things. The maximum penalty for trafficking is imprisonment for life.

In an unusual arrangement, a person accused of trafficking must first be convicted of possession. Then it is up to the accused to introduce evidence to show that he did not have possession for the purpose of trafficking. The Crown may introduce evidence adducing that the accused did have possession for the purpose of trafficking.

A person convicted for possession, who is himself a drug addict, may be placed in preventive detention for medical treatment for an indefinite period of time.

The flow of narcotics into Canada is mostly from the United States. The minimum penalty for smuggling narcotics into Canada is seven years imprisonment.

Whether or not Parliament will agree to "legalize pot" some-time in the future is something which will require strong debate. Much of the controversy centres on medical questions which are still unanswered. Commissions and research groups have been set up to try and determine if there are harmful results from marijuana use. Those who favour legalized marijuana are certain no one will be able to produce a report condemning marijuana on health grounds because they have tried it and found it harmless to date. If the medical evidence points to harmful results from prolonged use, many users will change their line of attack and say, "So are cigarettes dangerous to health." Opponents to legalized marijuana traditionally draw the line at the word "drug". They see no distinction between any type of drug—except for the ones prescribed by doctors, all drugs are bad. Many persons simply cannot understand why anyone would want marijuana. If it is so mild and harmless, how can it be all that effective? There are many excellent publications available concerning marijuana, and the reader should avail himself of those if he is genuinely interested in further study of the drug itself.

One suggestion that is often made is that marijuana should be sold through government outlets similar to liquor stores. Some people believe the price would come down. This idea should be examined again in the light of other controlled com-modities, such as tobacco and alcohol. The prices of these commodities have remained very high because of government taxes on them.

Nearly every country in the world is concerned about drug problems. Turkey eliminated about 50% of its poppy production in 1972. Mexico imposes an automatic five year prison sentence for marijuana possession. About three hundred Americans and Canadians are serving sentences in Mexican jails on drug charges.

For many persons, drug possession and use is part of a vast game, somewhat along the lines of a cops and robbers thriller that brings a sense of adventure in outwitting the RCMP, parents and teachers. Unfortunately, the game can bring arrest and a criminal record at a very early age. A criminal record shuts hundreds of doors—tightly and permanently. Jobs of importance and responsibility require bond, which a person with a criminal record cannot get. Government positions, particularly those requiring a security check, are out. Police work is fairly well out. Regardless of their stand for or against drug use or its legalization, citizens must recognize that the law at present prohibits drug use, and that violators may be penalized more in later life than they realize at the moment. When prohibition came in, many men quietly went into the basement and poured their beer and whiskey down the drain. It wasn't that they'd taken a sudden dislike to alcohol, but the law of the land had been changed and they accepted that. Other men went immediately to work making beer and whiskey as fast as they could. The law of the land had been changed and they were going to make a killing. Society needs more of the former and fewer of the latter to survive.

POINTS TO PONDER

1. Should marijuana be legalized under government controls?

2. What evidence is necessary to prove trafficking?

3. Codeine is contained in some cough syrups. Would possession of a large supply of cough syrup be a drug offence?

PROJECT

Conduct a survey among friends, relatives, and other acquaintances regarding this question:

Should Canada legalize marijuana?

Try to get a reasonable cross-section of persons by age, sex, occupation, and social class. Aim for at least fifty responses. It may be more interesting to separate answers by age groups, such as under 18, 18-30, and over 30. Compile your answers along the following lines:

RESPONSES

For Legalized Marijuana		*Against Legalized Marijuana*	
Reasons	*No.*	*Reasons*	*No.*
No evidence of health danger		It is harmful to health	
It will be used anyway		It will be too plentiful	
A matter of personal choice		Leads to use of hard drugs	
Other: Specify		Other: Specify	

Comments

Extortion

To "extort" means to "force out of". Extortion is forcing something of value from someone, whether it be forcing payment, an act, or a favour he would otherwise decline to give. The Criminal Code states:

305. (1) Everyone who, without reasonable justification or excuse and with intent to extort or gain anything, by threats, accusations, menaces or violence induces or attempts to induce any person, whether or not he is the person threatened, accused or menaced or to whom violence is shown, to do anything or to cause anything to be done, is guilty of an indictable offence and is liable to imprisonment for fourteen years.

(2) A threat to institute civil proceedings is not a threat for the purpose of this section.

A man entered Canada illegally from Portugal, obtained a job, and started work. Another man learned about this and threatened to tell the Immigration Department the facts unless the worker paid him $20 a week to keep quiet. The worker was eventually caught and deported back to Portugal. Before he left, he told about the man who had been extorting money from him. The man was convicted of extortion.

A man was involved in an automobile accident with another motorist. Each time he tried to contact the other driver about payment of damages, he received no reply. He finally sent a registered letter stating that unless he received payment within two weeks, he would file a civil law suit for damages. This was not a case of extortion, since the only statement made was that a civil law suit would be initiated.

Extortion has several other names, such as blackmail, shakedown, or bite. The maximum penalty is ten years imprisonment.

POINTS TO PONDER

1. If a judge ordered a person to pay a fine or go to jail for an offence, would this be extortion?

2. A doctor is told to contribute to a fund-raising drive for a new hospital, and warned that if he doesn't do so, he will not be allowed to use the facilities in the new hospital. Is this extortion?

Firearms and Offensive Weapons

The control of guns and other weapons is a big problem for police in most parts of the world. In many countries no one may own a gun, so the problem is solved before it starts. In the United States, there are so many guns that some families have ten or more. The state of Texas still permits a man to wear a gun.

After the gun slayings of President John Kennedy, Robert Kennedy, and Martin Luther King, strong sentiment arose in Congress to license all guns and outlaw small pistols entirely. These efforts were not successful, mostly because of the strong protest from the National Rifle Association. The American public declared that it wants guns—for pleasure and for self-protection.

Canada does not have a gun problem of nearly the size of the American one. Firstly, we do not have the population, and secondly, Canadians prefer hunting weapons to pistols. The law regarding weapons is somewhat complex and will require considerable explanation.

PROHIBITED WEAPONS

Some weapons are totally illegal and may not be possessed by anyone. These are classed by the Criminal Code as prohibited weapons, and include:

Any device to muffle the sound of a firearm, such as a gun silencer.

Any knife that opens by spring, gravity, or centrifugal force, such as a switchblade knife.

A weapon of any kind declared by order of the governor in council as a prohibited weapon.

The maximum penalty for possession of a prohibited weapon is five years imprisonment.

RESTRICTED WEAPONS

Other weapons are not illegal, but strict controls are exercised over them. Restricted weapons are:

Any firearm designed, altered, or intended to be aimed and fired by the action of one hand, such as a hand gun or pistol.

Any firearm capable of firing bullets in rapid succession during one pressure of the trigger, such as an automatic rifle.

Any firearm less than 26 inches in length, whether this is the length of the entire weapon or is achieved by folding or tele-scoping, such as a rifle with folding stock.

Any eligible person who wants to buy a restricted weapon must first get a police permit. The police will refuse a permit to anyone who is under age, has a criminal record, is mentally impaired, is intoxicated, or cannot give a valid reason for wanting the gun. Once the permit is acquired, the person may buy the weapon, whether from a store or from a private seller. He must then take the gun back to the police and register it. He must not lend the gun, or sell it without another permit.

Some of the offences concerning restricted weapons are listed below. Each carries a maximum penalty of two years imprisonment.

Failure to register a weapon
Lending a weapon without a permit
Possession of a weapon outside a dwelling house
Having a restricted weapon in a motor vehicle
Carrying a concealed weapon

Generally, small hand guns and other restricted weapons are more of a nuisance than of any value. About the only place you may keep them is in your home or at a gun club. If you go out in your yard and shoot at a can, you violate the law. Put it in your car and drive out to a remote spot to plink at something, and you commit two offences. Since there is not much chance for enjoyment with such guns, it is better not to own one.

OTHER WEAPONS

Hunting rifles, shotguns, and ammunition may be purchased by anyone over the age of sixteen. This age limit might seem rather low, but bear in mind that traditionally young Canadians hunted to supplement their family's food supply. Even now to require an age limit of eighteen or higher would cause hardship for some families who rely upon these young hunters.

In some municipalities, it is possible for someone as young as fourteen to get a permit to hunt with a gun. Special permission *is* required, however.

Anyone who sells or lends a gun to someone under the age of sixteen is guilty of an offence punishable on summary conviction.

Hunter safety must be stressed by everyone, of whatever age. Anyone who points a weapon at another person or handles it in a manner that is dangerous to others, is guilty of an offence punishable by up to two years imprisonment. As discussed in the section on assault, shooting at another person with intent to hit them is punishable by up to fourteen years imprisonment.

If you should need a firearm for any purpose exercise safety and good judgement at all times.

POINTS TO PONDER

1. A man takes his twelve-year-old son hunting. Both have shotguns. When a game warden comes near, the man is holding both guns. Would a conviction be possible?

2. A man is target shooting with a rifle and lets his fourteen-year-old son take a few pot shots now and then. Discuss the legality of this.

3. The Criminal Code says a firearm is any barrelled weapon that propels a missile at a speed of 500 feet or more per second. How would a CO_2 pistol be rated? Check with your local sporting goods store.

4. Police raid a house looking for drugs, and find none. They find a handgun which is not registered. Can they arrest the man and seize the gun if it is not mentioned on the search warrant? Check the section on civil rights and individual safeguards.

Forgery

324. (1) Every one commits forgery who makes a false document, knowing it to be false, with intent

(a) that it should be in any way used or acted upon as genuine, to the prejudice of any one whether within Canada or not, or

(b) that some person should be induced by the belief that it is genuine, to do or to refrain doing anything, whether within Canada or not.

There is no limit to the variety of things that people forge for personal profit. They include, but are not limited to, the following:

Bills of Exchange
Passports
Signatures
Wills
Contracts
Historical Documents
Land Titles
Trade Marks
Official Seals
Telegrams
Rare Stamps
Stocks and Bonds
Death Certificates
Birth Certificates
Visas
Marriage Records
Social Insurance Records
Credit Cards
Money Orders

The maximum penalty for forgery is fourteen years imprisonment.

With modern photographic and printing methods, forgery is becoming one of the easiest crimes to commit. Expert forgers can make perfect copies of anything, right down to using exactly the same type of paper. The best defence against forgers is to know with whom you are doing business.

A well-dressed man opened a bank account in a Toronto bank. He conducted a lot of cash transactions through the account for several months. Then, he approached the manager and asked for a loan of $15,000. He promised to secure the loan with Ontario Hydro Bonds as collateral. After receiving a $15,000 loan for which he put up $20,000 in bonds, he cleaned out his bank account and vanished. The bonds which the bank held turned out to be forgeries—counterfeit. They were such perfect reproductions only experts were able to detect the small flaws.

In addition to making a false document, it is also forgery to alter a real document.

A man held a savings bond that matured on August 1, 1974. Being in the need of money, he erased the last numbers and typed in 1971. This meant the bond could be cashed for its full value any time after August 1, 1971. When he tried to cash it, the alteration was detected and he was arrested for forgery.

POINTS TO PONDER

1. A man received a driver's licence with his name spelt wrongly. He corrected the spelling by erasing and typing his name correctly. Is this forgery? Carry this further—could he be charged for doing the same thing to other documents such as marriage certificates, credit cards, etc., if he thought he was *correcting* them?

2. A busy employer tells his secretary to sign letters for him. She signs them, attempting to copy his signature as best she can. Is this forgery? Explain your answer.

Fraud

Fraud is a very difficult subject to pin down, since it is mentioned in dozens of sections throughout the Criminal Code. To succeed in a charge of fraud, the Crown must be able to prove three things:

That a material misrepresentation has taken place and that the defrauded party acted upon it.

That the defrauded party actually suffered a loss.

That the fraud was intentional and/or made with reckless disregard for the truth.

Intent is very important in a fraud case. For example, if a man sells a bond to a client knowing that it is worthless, his intent is to cheat or defraud the victim. If he sells a bond to a client not knowing that there is anything wrong with it, fraud cannot be proven.

For our purposes, rather than attempt to discuss all forms of fraud, it would be perhaps best to discuss only one section as an example.

355. (1) Every one who, with intent to defraud,

(a) destroys, mutilates, alters, falsifies, or makes a false entry in, or

(b) omits a material particular form, or alters a material particular in,

a book, paper, writing, valuable security or document is guilty of an indictable offence and is liable to imprisonment for five years.

(2) Every one who, with intent to defraud his creditors, is privy to the commission of an offence under subsection (1) is guilty of an indictable offence and is liable to imprisonment for five years.

A Toronto man wanted to sell his small business, which was losing money. He was sure no buyer would offer much for the

100

business, so he set about altering the company books to make it appear the company was doing well. He got the cooperation of the bookkeeper by offering him 10% of the inflated price the business would bring. The two men began to enter false information in the books. Inventories were exaggerated over their true values. Bank accounts were inflated with imaginary entries. Sales were increased on paper only. The fraudulent books made the company appear to be making an excellent profit and growing each year. The owner then sold the company to a buyer, then he and the bookkeeper left town. The new owner ordered an audit and found he had been defrauded of nearly $200,000. The two culprits were caught and sent to prison.

Fraud normally takes the form of some kind of falsifying of books or documents. Another common method is to bill someone for work never done, impersonate someone, keep false accounts under assumed names, forge trade marks, false labelling or putting greatly exaggerated price tags on items, and countless others. Penalties range from fines on summary conviction to fourteen years imprisonment.

POINTS TO PONDER

1. A man sells a car to another man. The sale takes place in Ontario, where all used cars sold must be accompanied by a Certificate of Mechanical Fitness which must be signed by a licensed mechanic certifying that the vehicle is safe and has passed his inspection. The seller gives the buyer such a certificate, but this certificate was obtained from a friend of his who was a mechanic but who never really checked the car at all. Is this fraud?

2. A jeweller sells a diamond ring to a customer, not telling him that it is second-hand. The jeweller had sold it once and then repossessed it from a customer who did not make his payments. Now he polishes up the small scratches on the gold and sells it again as new. Is this fraud?

Habitual Criminals and Preventive Detention

While interviewing the assistant warden of a large prison, I asked him, "Are some inmates incorrigible?" He replied that they were. No matter how hard officials tried, some persons are bound to live by crime all their lives. What can society do about persons who will commit crimes every chance they get? Is there no safeguard against criminals who are not the least bit affected by the time they have already spent in prison? There is.

688. (1) Where an accused has been convicted of an indictable offence the court may, upon application, impose a sentence of preventive detention in lieu of any other sentence that might be imposed for the offence of which he was convicted or that was imposed for such offence, or in addition to any sentence that was imposed for such offence if the sentence has expired, if

(a) the accused is found to be an habitual criminal, and

(b) the court is of the opinion that because the accused is an habitual criminal, it is expedient for the protection of the public to sentence him to preventive detention.

(2) For the purposes of subsection (1), an accused is an habitual criminal if

(a) he has previously, since attaining the age of eighteen years, on at least three separate and independent occasions been convicted of an indictable offence for which he was liable to imprisonment for five years or more and is leading persistently a criminal life, or

(b) he has previously been sentenced to preventive detention.

"Preventive Detention" means detention in a penitentiary for an indeterminate period.

The assistant warden also told me that preventive detention is the sentence inmates hate most. Unlike other convicts who can count the days until they are released, the habitual criminal doesn't know if or when he will ever get out. In review, to be sentenced to preventive detention, a person must have:

Been convicted three times before to an indictable offence, for which the punishment *could* have been five years imprisonment or more—even though the sentence he actually received might not have been of that length, or

Have been sentenced to preventive detention before.

A man convicted of armed robbery was found to have been convicted of armed robbery on two previous occasions, and also convicted for assault with a weapon on one other occasion. The judge sentenced him to preventive detention for an indeterminate period, declaring him to be an habitual criminal.

Dangerous sexual offenders may also be sentenced to preventive detention.

How does an inmate serving such an indeterminate sentence ever get released? The Solicitor General of Canada must review, at least once each year, the condition, history, and circumstances of that person for the purpose of determining whether he should be permitted to be at large on licence, and if so, on what conditions. This duty is actually carried out by the National Parole Board.

So we see that the only way an inmate can hope for release from preventive detention is to convince the Parole Board that he is now able to lead a lawful life; that he will no longer commit offences. For a person convicted at least four times of indictable offences, this will take some convincing! Hence the saying among inmates: "Never be a three-time loser."

POINTS TO PONDER

1. A man had been in prison three times for long terms on indictable offences. He was released, and a year later was arrested on a driving charge. Should he be returned to prison as a habitual criminal because of this charge for dangerous driving?

2. Can a person who is imprisoned as a habitual criminal apply for parole like other inmates?

3. Should the Crown be allowed to appeal if a judge refuses to sentence a person as an habitual criminal?

4. Read again the explanation of preventive detention. Why not sentence all offenders to indefinite terms and release them only when they are reformed and apparently ready to lead a law-abiding life?

5. Canada copied the idea of preventive detention from Great Britain. Today, certain groups in Canada are arguing that preventive detention should be done away with as it is cruel and it violates a person's rights to put him in prison for an indefinite term. Do you agree that preventive detention should be removed from the Criminal Code?

Incest

Laws were passed against incest long ago because man realized very early that children of blood relatives were often abnormal and particularly prone to mental problems. Each person has an inherited propensity for certain diseases and other disorders. If two closely-related persons have children, then the chance that these children will be deformed or retarded is much greater. The Criminal Code states:

150. (1) Every one commits incest who, knowing that another person is by blood relationship his or her parent, child, brother, sister, grandparent or grandchild, as the case may be, has sexual intercourse with that person.

(2) Every one who commits incest is guilty of an indictable offence and is liable to imprisonment for fourteen years, and in the case of a male person is liable, in addition, to be whipped.

(3) Where a female person is convicted of an offence under this section and the court is satisfied that she committed the offence by reason only that she was under restraint, duress or fear of the person with whom she had the sexual intercourse, the court is not required to impose any punishment on her.

(4) In this section, "brother" and "sister", respectively, include half-brother and half-sister.

A man in British Columbia was charged with incest for knowingly marrying his natural mother, although they had not seen each other since the man was born. The couple pleaded guilty to bigamy, since the man already had another wife, and the charge of incest was dropped.

POINTS TO PONDER

1. In postwar Germany, couples who wanted to marry had to present to the registrar a family tree. The situation was chaotic because the war had disrupted families, men were missing, and refugees were moving around in large numbers. What was the reason for this strict requirement that couples provide the registrar with a complete family tree, back at least two generations?

2. Incest is discussed thoroughly in the Bible as unnatural and offensive to God. Most reported cases involve persons living in areas so remote that normal contact with others outside the immediate family is cut off. Certain nations may owe their existence today to incest in some form, since the early beginnings may have been little more than one family. Rulers in various nations practised incest because they believed their family line was superior or even divine and wanted to preserve it. Is the opposition today social, moral, or medical?

Indecent Acts and Obscene Matter

It is very difficult to define what is obscene or indecent. To one person, a particular picture or expression may be indecent. Another person may find it difficult to make up his mind. A third person may find the same things quite harmless. Decency means different things to different persons. The Criminal Code establishes a general rule that anything which has as its purpose,

The undue exploitation of sex, or of sex and any one or more of the following subjects, namely, crime, horror, cruelty and violence, shall be deemed to be obscene.

All publications and films are subject to this interpretation. However, getting a conviction is difficult because no one agrees upon what "undue exploitation" is.

A magazine in Toronto had a photograph of a woman giving birth to a child on the cover. A charge was filed claiming that the photo was an undue exploitation of sex. The defence got testimony from several ministers of different faiths that they did not find the photograph obscene. The charge was dismissed.

Another test is to ask whether the purpose of the publication or act is for the public good, or whether it was meant to be disgusting and offensive in nature. This rule is not easily enforced, either. Another ambiguous section in the Code reads:

169. Every one who wilfully does an indecent act

(a) in a public place in the presence of one or more persons, or

(b) in any place, with intent thereby to insult or offend any person,

is guilty of an offence punishable on summary conviction.

Again, what is an indecent act? The Criminal Code does prohibit appearing nude in public, or swearing. However, it would appear that each case must be examined on its own circumstances in order to try and reach a verdict.

POINTS TO PONDER

1. If the "undue exploitation of sex" is deemed to be obscene, how do films which are rated Adult Only escape the law?

2. Check your local newsstand and evaluate some of the magazines and books as being "undue exploitation of sex." What do you find?

3. Certain gestures made with the hand or fingers are universally understood to be obscene in their meaning. If these gestures are made publicly, would this constitute an indecent act under the wording of the section?

Kidnapping and Abduction

Kidnapping is an old form of extortion that has been known to this world for many years. It was seldom aimed at children, but more often at rivals. For example, in the 1920's large cities experienced the growth of gangs involved in organized and often violent crime. Kidnapping between rival gangs was common. The idea was to kidnap the leader of the other gang and make the gang pay to get him back. Gangster grabbed gangster, but the public was not involved and the police were seldom called in. Then kidnapping became an amateur crime, and the victims were children, not gangsters. Stealing children and making their parents pay to get them back was far more ruthless than the war that took place between criminal elements. In 1936 the son of Charles Lindberg, the first man to fly the Atlantic, was kidnapped. The boy was killed even though the ransom was paid, and there was a public outcry urging the authorities to be ruthless with kidnappers. Canada views the offence no less strongly than any nation in the world.

247. (1) Every one who kidnaps a person with intent

(a) to cause him to be confined or imprisoned against his will,

(b) to cause him to be unlawfully sent or transported out of Canada against his will, or

(c) to hold him for ransom or to service against his will,

is guilty of an indictable offence and is liable to imprisonment for life.

(2) Every one who, without lawful authority, confines, imprisons or forcibly seizes another person is guilty of an indictable offence and is liable to imprisonment for five years.

(3) In proceedings under this section the fact that the person in relation to whom the offence is alleged to have been committed did not resist is not a defence unless the accused proves that the failure to resist was not caused by threats, duress, force or exhibition of force.

248. Every one who takes away or detains a female person against her will, with intent

(a) to marry her or to have illicit sexual intercourse with her, or

(b) to cause her to marry or to have illicit sexual intercourse with a male person,

is guilty of an indictable offence and is liable to imprisonment for ten years.

249. (1) Every one who, without lawful authority, takes or causes to be taken an unmarried female person under the age of sixteen years out of the possession of and against the will of her parent or guardian or of any other person who has lawful care or charge of her is guilty of an indictable offence and is liable to imprisonment for five years.

(2) For the purpose of proceedings under this section it is not material whether

(a) the female person is taken with her own consent or at her own suggestion, or

(b) the accused believes that the female person is sixteen years of age or more.

250. (1) Every one who, with intent to deprive a parent or guardian or any other person who has lawful care or charge of a child under the age of fourteen years of the possession of that child, or with intent to steal anything on or about the person of such a child, unlawfully

(a) takes or entices away or detains the child, or

(b) receives or harbours the child,

is guilty of an indictable offence and is liable to imprisonment for ten years.

(2) This section does not apply to a person who, claiming in good faith a right to possession of a child, obtains possession of the child.

A woman who could not bear a child of her own, entered a hospital and put on a nurse's gown. Then she went to the maternity ward and entered a room where a woman was nursing her baby. She said, "Time for the baby to go back to the nursery," and then left the hospital with the baby. When she was found she claimed the baby was her own. She faced a ten-year sentence, but was found mentally unfit to stand trial and committed to a mental hospital.

A young man of eighteen had a girlfriend who was fifteen. He told her he was going out west to look for a job. She said she was bored with school and her home life and asked him to take her with him. *They went to Alberta in his car and lived together for six weeks before the police found them. The man was charged with abduction, even though the girl had suggested the whole thing. Both contended nothing intimate had occurred during their time together; if anything the man had looked after the girl like a big brother and kept her from possible harm had she fallen in with someone else. He received a suspended sentence and the girl was returned to her home.*

A boy of thirteen ran away from home and went to Toronto where he knew some older boys who were living in a hippie commune. They greeted him and took him into their living quarters. When the police found the missing boy, they charged his two older friends for "harbouring" the boy knowing all the while he was away illegally from his parents.

POINTS TO PONDER

1. Two parents obtained a divorce and the court ordered custody of their child to be given to the mother. Later the father picked the child up at school and left the province with him. How does such an act fit under the meaning of this section?

2. A male, aged seventeen, is arrested for living with a female, aged fifteen. She has told him she is seventeen. He is charged with taking her out of the custody of her parents against their wishes. Examine this case in the light of the wording of section 249. If the two youngsters both insist that there was nothing intimate in their relationship, would this have a bearing on the outcome of the case?

3. If in a similar case, one parent consented to the taking away but the other did not because he or she wasn't informed, could the second parent bring a charge? What is the meaning of the act when it says "parent"? Both parents, or just the father? Either?

4. What would be the outcome if parental permission were obtained by deceit, that the parents were falsely told the purpose of the taking away?

Man Traps

Assume that a cottage owner had constant trouble with thieves breaking into his cottage, particularly during the winter months. These thefts were becoming costly, and sometimes the thieves wrecked the cottage, committing vandalism as well as theft. One fall he closed his cottage as usual, but with one exception. He rigged a shotgun fastened to a chair, connected by a pulley to the front door. The apparatus would fire a shotgun blast at the first person who opened the door. Was he within his rights to protect his property by setting such traps?

> 231. (1) Every one who, with intent to cause death or bodily harm to persons, whether ascertained or not, sets or places or causes to be set or placed a trap, device or other thing whatsoever that is likely to cause death or bodily harm to persons is guilty of an indictable offence and is liable to imprisonment for five years.
>
> (2) A person who, being in occupation or possession of a place where anything mentioned in subsection (1) has been set or placed, knowingly and wilfully permits it to remain there, shall be deemed, for the purposes of that subsection, to have set or placed it with the intent mentioned therein.

You might assume that a person should have the right to protect his property by setting devices to discourage thieves. As far as the law is concerned, this is wrong because one may only use the degree of force necessary to protect one's property. One cannot know in advance what is going to be necessary. Traps are indiscriminate. It is easily conceivable that someone might have cause to enter the property for a legitimate reason and be killed by a trap left for thieves. For example, if a fire broke out in the cottage and a fireman forced the door open to fight the fire, he would be killed while entering the cottage for a perfectly valid reason. Consider, too, that if traps were allowed, then homes, businesses, and nearly every kind of building would be rigged with traps. No one could with safety go near a building because it might contain traps. Forgetful people would set off their own traps and kill themselves. The traps might be faulty and go off prematurely and injure anyone nearby. Curious children would set traps off at an alarming rate.

Traps, then, must be ruled out as a legitimate way to protect property.

POINTS TO PONDER

1. Would leaving a vicious dog inside a premises without any warning sign constitute setting a man trap? Explain your answer.

2. Suppose that a farmer, annoyed by snowmobiles crossing his land, strung a wire fence between some trees. If it caused injury, who would bear the burden of proof? Would the Crown have to prove it was a man trap and had no other purpose, or would the defence have to prove it was a fence, not a trap, and had a valid reason to be there?

Manslaughter

Killing another person is classed as "culpable homicide." This term means "the killing of a person for which another person is accountable." It is the circumstances of a case which decide whether the homicide is murder or manslaughter. Murder is discussed separately in this text.

215. (1) Culpable homicide that otherwise would be murder may be reduced to manslaughter if the person who committed it did so in the heat of passion caused by sudden provocation.

(2) A wrongful act or insult that is of such a nature as to be sufficient to deprive an ordinary person of the power of self-control is provocation for the purposes of this section if the accused acted upon it on the sudden and before there was time for his passion to cool.

(3) For the purposes of this section the questions

(a) whether a particular wrongful act or insult amounted to provocation, and

(b) whether the accused was deprived of the power of self-control by the provocation that he alleges he received,

are questions of fact, but no one shall be deemed to have given provocation to another by doing anything that he had a legal right to do, or by doing anything that the accused incited him to do in order to provide the accused with an excuse for causing death or bodily harm to any human being.

(4) Culpable homicide that otherwise would be murder is not necessarily manslaughter by reason only that it was committed by a person who was being arrested illegally, but the fact that the illegality of the arrest was known to the accused may be evidence of provocation for the purposes of this section.

217. Culpable homicide that is not murder or infanticide is manslaughter.

219. Everyone who commits manslaughter is guilty of an indictable offence and is liable to imprisonment for life.

Manslaughter is often thought of as a lesser offence which is included in murder. This means that although the prosecution may ask for conviction for murder, the jury has the choice of finding the accused not guilty of murder, but guilty of manslaughter, a lesser and included offence.

The question of provocation is an important one. Murder is assumed to be a careful plan to kill someone. There should at least be evidence that the murderer intended to kill his victim. Manslaughter may result from a sudden disagreement, loss of temper or self-control, when the slayer may not have intended death or even severe harm at all. Often, remorse sets in immediately when the slayer realizes that he has over-reacted and killed his adversary.

Two men exchanged words at a bar. One called the other a very vile name. The second man angrily punched the first man solidly in the chest above the heart. The blow ruptured the heart and caused death. The charge laid was manslaughter, not murder, since there was no evidence that the slayer intended to kill the victim, but merely over-reacted to the provocation.

Note that provocation does not *excuse* the slayer, but only shows that murder was not his intention. In some American cases, extreme provocation has been termed "temporary insanity" and the defendant has been found not guilty. Canadian courts have not been as willing to accept this plea as complete justification for a culpable homicide.

A man was dismissed from his job by his employer. He drove home, brooded a while, drank a lot, then went back to work with a gun. He barged into his employer's office and shot him to death, wounded three other persons, then shot it out with police for several hours. When finally captured, he was brought to trial for murder. His plea of provocation was rejected. The court ruled that since he had ample time to go home and let his passion cool, his offence was not a reaction to provocation, but one of intent to kill his employer.

The question as to who or what caused death can become an involved one if the death is not immediate.

> 210. No person commits culpable homicide or the offence of causing the death of a human being by criminal negligence unless the death occurs within one year and one day commencing with the time of the occurrence of the last event by means of which he caused or contributed to the cause of death.

Thus, if medical technology can manage to keep the victim alive for a year and a day, before he dies, then no one can be convicted for causing his death.

Another problem arises when death results from another cause but is aggravated by the injury. Usually the attacker is still held responsible. This can happen in several possible ways:

The injury so weakens the victim that he dies from an intervening, subsequent disease, such as pneumonia.

After injury, the victim must undergo medical treatment or an operation that is dangerous by itself, and subsequently dies from the effects of the operation.

The victim already suffers from a serious disease and the injury accelerates death.

A person commits homicide by failing to prevent a death which he had the proper means to prevent, if he had resorted to those means.

The following examples illustrate some of the points mentioned.

Regina v. Smith (1959)
A man stabbed another man twice. Friends of the victim carried him to a medical centre, but dropped him several times while doing so. He subsequently died, as a result of both the knife wounds and the excessive bleeding caused by having been dropped. His death was attributed to the person who stabbed him.

Regina v. Jordan (1956)
The victim was stabbed by the accused and committed to hospital. He was given an injection of terramycin to prevent infection from the stab wound. Some people are intolerant to terramycin and develop complications. The victim reacted to the terramycin and subsequently died. The death was still considered the fault of the man who stabbed him.

Regina v. Allen (1954)
The accused struck the deceased man on the jaw. Unknown to him, the man had a severe bone disease which had already weakened the jaw bone greatly. The blow, which would ordin-arily not cause severe injury to a healthy man, shattered the victim's jaw terribly and thrust a section of broken bone into the brain causing death. Although the attacker did not know about the condition of his victim, he was held liable for his death.

Regina v. Mowrey (1958)
The captain of a small ship was informed that a man had fallen overboard. He refused all requests to turn about and conduct a search for the man on the grounds that it was hopeless since the water temperature was so low that survival was impossible. Charges were brought against the captain for failing to prevent a death when he had the means to do so. The jury was dead-locked and the case not retried.

From the foregoing, we see that homicide is a serious offence and persons indulging in violent activities, such as assault, may find themselves in more serious trouble than they expect. It does not excuse the offence just because the victim has a "glass jaw" and the attacker does not know it, or pneumonia sets in and the victim dies, although the attacker does not foresee it; it is still culpable homicide. Our law holds that a death which is brought about by another person, although indirectly, may still be attributed to him.

One instance where stricter enforcement of our law is needed is in the area of hunting fatalities. Quite often, hunters are fatally shot by other hunters, and yet no charges are brought. The tendency to excuse this kind of "accident" does little to prevent similar careless shootings.

POINTS TO PONDER

1. A point of law requires that in order to prove murder, *intent* must be proved by the Crown. The Crown does not have to prove intent for a conviction for manslaughter. Why is there this difference?

2. A man, whose wife was raped, sought out the wrongdoer and killed him. Would he succeed in a defence of provocation?

3. In a 1957 appeal case, *Lowther v. Regina*, the accused Lowther had been abused, terrorized and threatened by the man he killed for over a year and a half prior to the slaying. Attempts to stop the threats by legal means had failed, so he finally resorted to violence. Discuss his situation in light of the meaning of provocation.

Masks

Criminals have reason to take measures against being identified. Their victims may know them. Police files may contain their photographs from previous arrests, and police artists can sketch excellent likenesses from witnesses' descriptions. The classic solution offenders use is to wear a mask. More cunning persons use theatre make-up and contrivances such as wigs, false moustaches, etc.

> 309. (2) Every one who, with intent to commit an indictable offence has his face masked or coloured or is otherwise disguised is guilty of an indictable offence and is liable to imprisonment for ten years.

Police received an anonymous tip that a milk store would be robbed at closing time. They staked out the store and at 10:00 p.m. two men entered wearing stockings over their heads. They surrendered meekly to the squad of police hidden in the store. They were convicted on separate counts for (1) attempted robbery, (2) illegal possession of a restricted weapon, and (3) wearing masks with intent to commit an indictable offence.

POINTS TO PONDER

1. Would you term a ten-year sentence for wearing a mask with intent to commit an indictable offence too severe? Compare, for example, with assault causing bodily harm which carries only a two-year penalty.

2. If a person committed a robbery on Hallowe'en night while wearing a costume, could he still be convicted under this section? Explain your answer.

3. Would such things as false moustaches or sideburns or false hair colouring be included as masks?

Murder

Student lawyers have often been asked on examinations to, "Define murder." Books have been written debating the issue, and many court cases have hinged on the question, "Was it murder?"

212. Culpable homicide is murder

(a) where the person who causes the death of a human being

(i) means to cause his death, or

(ii) means to cause him bodily harm that he knows is likely to cause his death, and is reckless whether death ensues or not;

(b) where a person, meaning to cause death to a human being or meaning to cause him bodily harm that he knows is likely to cause his death, and being reckless whether death ensues or not, by accident or mistake causes death to another human being, notwithstanding that he does not mean to cause death or bodily harm to that human being; or

(c) where a person, for an unlawful object, does anything that he knows or ought to know is likely to cause death, and thereby causes death to a human being, notwithstanding that he desires to effect his object without causing death or bodily harm to any human being.

213. Culpable homicide is murder where a person causes the death of a human being while committing or attempting to commit treason or an offence mentioned in section 52 (sabotage), piracy, escape or rescue from prison or lawful custody, resisting lawful arrest, rape, indecent assault, forcible abduction, robbery, burglary or arson, whether or not the person means to cause death to any human being and whether or not he knows that death is likely to be caused to any human being, if

(a) he means to cause bodily harm for the purpose of

(i) facilitating the commision of the offence, or

(ii) facilitating his flight after committing or attempting to commit the offence,

and the death ensues from the bodily harm;

(b) he administers a stupefying or overpowering thing for a purpose mentioned in paragraph (a), and the death ensues therefrom;

(c) he wilfully stops, by any means, the breath of a human being for a purpose mentioned in paragraph (a), and the death ensues therefrom; or

(d) he uses a weapon or has it upon his person

(i) during or at the time he commits or attempts to commit the offence, or

(ii) during or at the time of his flight after committing or attempting to commit the offence,

and the death ensues as a consequence.

Note that the definition in section 212 says homicide is murder if either the death of the victim was intended, or bodily harm which might be fatal was likely. Also, if the wrong person is killed by mistake, it is still murder.

A man was separated from his wife and resented her family taking sides with her against him. He particularly blamed his mother-in-law for his marital troubles. He went to her home one night and shot at her through the window with a rifle. He missed his mother-in-law but killed her sister who was visiting. He was convicted of murder, although he missed his intended victim. The fact that he did not intend that the other woman should die was immaterial.

Note, too, that a death resulting during or from the commission of another offence is murder, whether death was intended or not. All parties to the first offence are considered parties to the murder.

Two men entered a store and robbed the store owner at gunpoint. As they started to leave the store, the owner reached under the counter and pulled out a gun. He shot one robber in the back, felling him. The other robber turned and shot the store owner. The store owner died, the wounded robber lived. Both men were charged with murder. The robber who killed the store owner had no defence. He had killed the man while committing an offence. The wounded robber pleaded as his defence that since he was shot down from behind, that he could not conceivably have been a party to the murder of the store owner, only the person who actually shot him was responsible. The court rejected this plea, holding that as a party to the robbery he must accept responsibility for the offence of murder as it arose out of the robbery, even though he did not shoot the store owner.

In another case, a man was charged with murder when his partner in a robbery was shot and killed by a policeman. The defence argued that the robber could not be held responsible for the death of his partner when the slaying had been already judged as justifiable homicide on the part of the policeman. The trial judge agreed. If the slaying of the robber was justifiable homicide by a policeman in the line of duty, then no one *could be later held liable for the homicide.*

Another aspect of murder is *mens rea*, or a knowledge of the wrongfulness of the act. It must be shown that the slayer intended the death of his victim, or at least was capable of formulating such an intent. Defences often hinge upon matters related to *mens rea*, such as insanity, drunkenness, provocation, and self-defence. This is perhaps what makes murder trials so sensational. Often the defence counsel does not try to argue that the accused did not slay the victim, but only that he did not commit murder because he could not intend to kill him.

One defence which is seldom acceptable is drunkenness. A person committing murder while drunk may claim that he did not know what he was doing. He may claim no recollection of the crime after it is over. The court does not often accept this defence. In most cases, the Crown contends that *drunkenness only affects the mind so that the person gives way more readily to some violent passion and does not rebut the presumption that the person intends the consequences of his act.* Thus, merely stating, "If I had been sober, I never would have done it," is not an adequate defence.

Regina v. Fisher (1961)
The accused was charged with murder of a woman to whom he had offered a ride after they had been drinking in a hotel beverage room. After they had indulged in a certain amount of fondling in his car, the accused took a sudden dislike to the woman and stabbed her fifteen times, then threw her body from the car. He later told police, "I really went off my rocker, I guess, or I must have been drunk, or a combination of both." The defence counsel argued that the accused was too drunk to be capable of forming an intent to kill the victim. The judge included in his instruction to the jury these words: "Now, the defence submits to you that the accused man was so drunk as to be unable to form the intent to commit murder. The defence, let me remind you, does not have to prove that. If there is any reasonable doubt in your mind, the accused man is entitled to the benefit of that doubt." The jury returned a verdict of guilty of murder.

Other defences that may be successful against a charge of murder are necessity, accident, and self-defence.

Regina v. Dudley and Stephens (1884)
This historic case involved two men and a boy adrift in a lifeboat at sea. When it became apparent that rescue was almost hopeless, the two men killed the boy and preserved their own lives by eating his flesh and drinking his blood. It was found that they killed him of necessity, not malice. They were acquitted of murder, and received only a short sentence for manslaughter.

A conviction for murder is possible although no specific intent is shown as to whom the victim was intended to be. It is sufficient to show that a general intent existed to murder someone.

A student climbed to the top of a large bell tower on the University of Texas campus. Without warning or apparent reason, he shot and killed eleven people on the campus with a high-powered rifle. He was convicted of murder, even though it could not be shown that he had a specific intent to kill the persons he did. It was enough to show that he had a general intent to kill someone or anyone.

While most murder in Canada is now punishable only by life imprisonment, the murder of a policeman or prison guard is capital murder. The judge *must* sentence the convicted person to death. This sentence can be commuted to life imprisonment by the federal cabinet.

Murder, as old as Cain killing Abel, is sometimes referred to as the most "human of crimes". It is doubtful that we shall ever be without it, for what is more natural than to want to kill those who offend us? Through social and moral education we attempt to convey to everyone that violent attacks upon others cannot solve problems, but only create greater ones. Most murders are family murders. Experienced police investigators will tell you that unless a murder has a political motive, such as assassination, or is committed in the course of another crime, the safest bet is to start looking in the same house for the killer. Seldom does a stranger commit murder. Almost always, the killer knew the victim and knew him very well.

POINTS TO PONDER

1. Define murder.

2. Manslaughter is an "included offence" of murder. What does this mean?

3. If a person kills another person, and claims it was accidental, is the burden of proof on him to prove it was an accident, or must the Crown prove it was not? If there were no witnesses, how will this be substantiated?

4. Presently in Canada, killing a policeman or prison guard is punishable by hanging. Killing anyone else is not. In the 1971 Kingston Penitentiary riot, two inmates were killed by other inmates because they were considered "undesirables". Six guards held hostage were not hurt. Would the difference in penalty for killing a guard versus killing an inmate be the reason why the guards were not harmed?

Negligence

Carelessness, recklessness, or indifference towards the lives and safety of others is not permissible. If another person is injured because of your careless behaviour, you may not dismiss the whole thing as an accident.

202. (1) Every one is criminally negligent who

(a) in doing anything, or

(b) in omitting to do anything that it is his duty to do,

shows wanton or reckless disregard for the lives or safety of other persons.

(2) For the purposes of this section, "duty" means a duty imposed by law.

203. Every one who by criminal negligence causes death to another person is guilty of an indictable offence and is liable to imprisonment for life.

204. Every one who by criminal negligence causes bodily harm to another person is guilty of an indictable offence and is liable to imprisonment for ten years.

In the section on automobile offences we touch upon criminal negligence with a motor vehicle, and probably most cases of negligence involve motor vehicles. However, negligence can occur in nearly any situation. Again, the problem of definition is very difficult.

One should not confuse negligence as a criminal offence with negligence as a civil tort (wrong). A lawsuit in which the plaintiff contends the defendant was negligent may be very different from a criminal charge arising from the same incident. In civil suits, the court may recognize *moral duty* as well as *duty imposed by law*.

Depue v. Flatau (1907)
Mr. Depue became ill while visiting Mr. Flatau on business.
Depue asked Flatau if he could remain in his home overnight.
Flatau refused and put Depue in his wagon, stuck the reins in
his hand, and started the horse homeward. It was a bitter cold
night and Depue fell from the wagon on the way home. He
suffered frostbite and nearly died. Depue sued Flatau. Flatau
argued that he had no duty imposed on him by law to take Mr.
Depue into his home. The court agreed that there was no such
duty imposed by law, but held that "failure to render assistance
in such a situation may constitute actionable negligence if the
injury is aggravated through lack of care."

Mr. Flatau was held to have not rendered an action which he
had a *moral duty* to do. For this, he paid damages in a civil
court. There is no indication that he could also be charged with
a criminal offence arising from the same incident, because the
criminal court only accepts as proof of criminal negligence a
duty imposed by law.

Another important difference between civil and criminal
cases regarding negligence is the matter of proof. In a civil
action, the proof may rest upon the defendant. This is a point
of law known as *res ipsa loquitur*, which means "the act speaks
for itself." If the injured party can show that although he is not
certain exactly how or why the defendant was negligent, but
surely he was somehow negligent, he may win his lawsuit just
on this probability. The defendant will have to prove he was not
negligent.

A truck delivering building supplies was parked next to an
apartment building under construction. Two men were unload-
ing lumber from the truck. Without warning, a large stack of
bricks fell from the top floor, causing head injuries to the two
men. They sued the contractor and the building owner for
damages for negligence. They could not prove who caused the
bricks to fall or why they fell, but claimed res ipsa
loquitur—*that they did not have to prove exactly why the*
bricks fell, but rather that it was obvious there was negligence

by the contractor or his workers, and therefore "the act speaks for itself." It would be the contractor's burder to prove he was not negligent.

This principle, *res ipsa loquitur,* has no bearing on a criminal case. There the burden of proof is always on the Crown. No criminal case could be successful based on the probability that the contractor was negligent. The Crown would have to prove exactly who caused the bricks to fall and how.

Having established the differences between civil and criminal negligence, let us turn attention to defining criminal negligence.

Would *mens rea* be a necessary element to prove criminal negligence? That is, if there was no malice aforethought or intent to carry out the negligent act, would criminal negligence be present? In Canadian courts, it has been so held. From an appeal case, *Regina v. Binus (1966)* comes this statement by the justice.

> By expressing criminal negligence in terms of recklessness it has been clearly shown that Parliament meant to retain one ingredient—the actual foresight of the particular accused as to the prohibited consequences of his conduct—as essential to conviction. This is *mens rea* in one of its two classical forms. The reckless man does not intend the result, but he foresees it may happen and then knowingly runs the risk of it happening.

From the learned justice's remarks we can see that criminal negligence is a violation of a duty imposed by law from which the accused person could foresee the consequences that might arise, whether he intended them or not, then continued his actions running the risk of those consequences without regard for the lives and safety of others.

A contractor who builds a grandstand for a fair uses defective materials to save costs. The grandstand collapses, killing several people, and the contractor is convicted of criminal negligence.

In the same situation, assume that the contractor builds the grandstand solidly, and informs the fair director that the grand-

132

stand can safely hold 600 people. The fair director authorizes 1,000 tickets to be sold for the grandstand. Under the weight of so many extra people, the grandstand collapses killing several people. The fair director is convicted of criminal negligence.

The reader should be reminded that it is not necessary that someone be actually injured or killed for a charge of criminal negligence to be brought. The charge may be brought for just allowing a dangerous situation to exist, whether anyone is harmed or not. The safest thing to do is to fulfil one's moral and legal duties to the utmost and thereby avoid either civil or criminal prosecution.

POINTS TO PONDER

1. It is generally considered difficult to prove criminal negligence. Why? What does wanton and reckless behaviour mean, and how can it be proved?

2. What would you consider to be the lawful duty of a person who drives a truck loaded with explosives?

3. Review the explanation of negligence under the section on automobile offences. If a person causes bodily harm while criminally negligent in the operation of a motor vehicle, which section and which penalty apply?

Robbery

It is sometimes hard to distinguish among the different offences which involve taking something of value from someone else. Words such as *steal, theft,* and *burglary* all seem to be used interchangeably. However, they do have slightly different meanings. *Robbery* assumes that the offender is armed and uses or threatens violence.

302. Every one commits robbery who

(a) steals, and for the purpose of extorting whatever is stolen or to prevent or overcome resistance to the stealing, uses violence or threats of violence to a person or property,

(b) steals from any person and, at the time he steals or immediately before or immediately thereafter, wounds, beats, strikes or uses any personal violence to that person,

(c) assaults any person with intent to steal from him, or

(d) steals from any person while armed with an offensive weapon or imitation thereof.

303. Every one who commits robbery is guilty of an indictable offence and is liable to imprisonment for life.

In each of the foregoing subsections, the threat or use of violence is very much a part of robbery. It is assumed that without such violence, the victim would refuse to be robbed. The severe punishment also reflects society's intense dislike of those who steal using violent means against honest citizens.

Armed robbery remains a serious problem. The ready availability of small guns despite legal restrictions, and the ease of holding up gas stations, small stores, and so forth, will continue to tempt thieves. The severe penalty which can be meted out for such a small gain should affect the logical processes of anyone considering such a crime.

POINTS TO PONDER

1. What differentiates robbery from theft?

2. If a person handed a note to the teller in a bank which read, "Put all your cash in this bag. I have a container of nitro-glycerine in my pocket. If you make a false move, I will set it off." Would this be armed robbery if it later turned out the person was bluffing? Explain your answer.

3. A man was robbed of his wallet by a thief who stood behind him and stuck his finger in the man's back and warned him not to turn around. The victim thought it was a gun. Was this armed robbery under section 302? Explain your answer.

4. A man who had a quarrel with another man beat him severely. As an afterthought, he stole his wallet. He was convicted of robbery, but appealed on the grounds that his real intent was assault not robbery, that he took the wallet on impulse only. How would you decide this appeal?

Sexual Offences

Policemen lament the amount of work they have to do enforcing moral laws. One commented, "All moral laws should be stricken from the books. Then the police could get down to the business of protecting property and maintaining public safety rather than snooping around in bedrooms."

Perhaps the removal of certain offences would make less work for the police, but it is not certain that the public safety would be enhanced. In some cases it is necessary for society to intervene, particularly when young people are involved. Women also require some special protection, if for no other reason than that they are generally physically weaker than men.

143. A male person commits rape when he has sexual intercourse with a female person who is not his wife,

(a) without her consent, or

(b) with her consent if the consent

(i)   is extorted by threats of fear of bodily harm,
(ii) is obtained by personating her husband, or
(iii) is obtained by false and fraudulent representations as to the nature and quality of the act.

144. Every one who commits rape is guilty of an indictable offence and is liable to imprisonment for life.

145. Every one who attempts to commit rape is guilty of an indictable offence and is liable to imprisonment for ten years.

Note that rape is deemed to have occurred regardless of how far penetration took place. Legally there is no such thing as a female person committing rape against a male person, although instances of this have taken place. These attacks can only be classed as assault. The law does not require the female person to resist violently, but only that she has not given consent. The male person *cannot* assume that because the female does not resist violently she consents. A husband cannot be convicted of rape of his wife whether she consents or not. Marriage gives him the automatic right to enjoy sexual relations with her.

The ages of persons involved in sexual relations is also a matter for the law.

146. (1) Every male person who has sexual intercourse with a female person who

(a) is not his wife, and

(b) is under the age of fourteen years,

whether or not he believes that she is fourteen years of age or more, is guilty of an indictable offence and is liable to imprisonment for life.

(2) Every male person who has sexual intercourse with a female person who

(a) is not his wife,

(b) is of previously chaste character, and

(c) is fourteen years of age or more and is under the age of sixteen years,

whether or not he believes that she is sixteen years of age or more, is guilty of an indictable offence and is liable to imprisonment for five years.

(3) Where an accused person is charged with an offence under subsection (2), the court may find the accused not guilty if it is of the opinion that the evidence does not show that, as between the accused and the female person, the accused is more to blame than the female person.

147. No male person shall be deemed to commit an offence under sections 144, 145, 146 or 150 while he is under the age of fourteen years.

A college student met a girl at a night beach party. He assumed that she too was a college student. Their evening led to drinking and sexual intercourse. She subsequently became ill from the amount of alcohol she had consumed and was taken home. Her parents took her to the hospital where doctors pumped out her stomach. They also treated her for profuse vaginal bleeding. The college student was arrested and convicted, since the girl was fifteen years of age. His ignorance of her true age was no excuse.

Note that "of previous chaste character" has been defined as a general feeling among "right-thinking" persons that there has been no prior evidence of impropriety or indecency in the girl's conduct.

149. (1) Every one who indecently assaults a female person is guilty of an indictable offence and is liable to imprisonment for five years.

(2) An accused who is charged with an offence under subsection (1) may be convicted if the evidence establishes that the accused did anything to the female person with her consent that, but for her consent, would have been an indecent assault, if her consent was obtained by false and fraudulent representations as to the nature and quality of the act.

151. Every male person who, being eighteen years of age or more, seduces a female person of previously chaste character who is sixteen years or more but less than eighteen years of age is guilty of an indictable offence and is liable to imprisonment for two years.

Tom was nineteen and his girlfriend Joan was seventeen. They began having sexual relations regularly. Later, Tom jilted Joan for another girl. Joan angrily charged him with her seduction for which he was convicted.

152. Every male person, being twenty-one years of age or more, who, under promise of marriage, seduces an unmarried female person of previously chaste character who is less than twenty-one years of age is guilty of an indictable offence and is liable to imprisonment for two years.

153. (1) Every male person who

(a) has illicit sexual intercourse with his step-daughter, foster daughter, or female ward; or

(b) has illicit sexual intercourse with a female person of previously chaste character and under the age of twenty-one years who

(i)   is in his employment,

(ii) is in a common, but not necessarily similar, employment with him and is, in respect of her employment or work, under or in any way subject to his control or direction, or

(iii) receives her wages or salary directly or indirectly from him,

140

is guilty of an indictable offence and is liable to imprisonment for two years.

(2) Where an accused is charged with an offence under paragraph (b) of subsection (1), the court may find the accused not guilty if it is of opinion that the evidence does not show that, as between the accused and the female person, the accused is more to blame than the female person.

The purpose of the preceding section may seem unclear. Generally, it was established to prevent male employers from using economic threats against female employees or male guardians from using their authority over girls in their charge in order to pursue sexual interests. The employer might indicate that refusal of the female employee would result in her being fired. The law makes such intercourse illegal under any guise— except of course if it was just as much her idea as his.

The next sections require some definition in advance. Rarely does the Criminal Code use a term without defining it. The somewhat puritan authors of the Code seem to have balked at defining the next terms, either because they think everyone understands them, or they think they are unmentionable.

Buggery is for a male person to have anal intercourse with another person, either male or female. (Also called sodomy.)

Bestiality is for a male person to commit unnatural sexual acts, such as intercourse, with an animal.

Gross indecency is any act suitable only in privacy which is committed in public without due regard for those who may view it.

155. Every one who commits buggery or bestiality is guilty of an indictable offence and is liable to imprisonment for fourteen years.

156. Every male person who assaults another person with intent to commit buggery or who indecently assaults another male person is guilty of an indictable offence and is liable to imprisonment for ten years.

157. Every one who commits an act of gross indencency with another person is guilty of an indictable offence and is liable to imprisonment for five years.

The sections dealing with buggery, bestiality, and gross indecency do not apply to husband and wife if committed in a private place. Unless this were so, certain acts committed in the privacy of married couples' bedrooms would be deemed crimes. However, no one may commit such acts in public. In 1970 a couple was arrested in Ottawa on a charge of gross indecency for allegedly having intercourse on the lawn of the National Arts Centre in the middle of the afternoon! Consenting adults over the age of twenty-one, whether married or not, also have no restrictions as long as the acts are done privately.

To many people, the sections concerning sexual offences are private matters and should not be contained in the Criminal Code at all, except perhaps for the section on rape. The general trend has been to lessen restrictions upon what people may do. Whether this will have a beneficial or harmful effect upon society in the long run still has to be seen.

POINTS TO PONDER

1. If a woman agrees to have intercourse with a man, and after commencing intercourse changes her mind and tells him to stop, would he be guilty of an offence if he refuses to do so?

2. If a man and a woman become engaged to marry and prior to their marriage have sexual relations, what possible charge can be brought against him if he breaks the engagement?

3. Several criminologists have linked the increase of sexual offences in the last decade to (a) the tremendous outpouring of pornographic books, magazines and movies, and (b) the trend of fashion towards such items as miniskirts. Discuss the validity of this observation.

Theft and Conversion

The law recognizes many forms of theft, and the punishment may vary according to who committed the theft and for what purpose. The general definition of theft is as follows:

283. (1) Every one commits theft who fraudulently and without colour of right takes, or fraudulently and without colour of right converts to his use or to the use of another person, anything whether animate or inanimate, with intent,

(a) to deprive, temporarily or absolutely, the owner of it or a person who has a special property or interest in it, of the thing or of his property or interest in it,

(b) to pledge it or deposit it as security,

(c) to part with it under a condition with respect to its return that the person who parts with it may be unable to perform, or

(d) to deal with it in such a manner that it cannot be restored in the condition in which it was at the time it was taken or converted.

(2) A person commits theft when, with intent to steal anything, he moves it or causes it to move or to be moved, or begins to cause it to become movable.

(3) A taking or conversion of anything may be fraudulent notwithstanding that it is effected without secrecy or attempt at concealment.

(4) For the purposes of this Act the question whether anything that is converted is taken for the purpose of conversion, or whether it is, at the time it is converted, in the lawful possession of the person who converts it is not material.

(5) For the purpose of this section a person who has a wild living creature in captivity shall be deemed to have a special property or interest in it while it is in captivity and after it has escaped from captivity.

A thief usually disposes of goods stolen for cash. If he chooses to keep something stolen for his own use, this is called conversion

A power mower disappeared from a man's tool shed. Several weeks later, he thought he saw it in another yard and called police. Armed with a search warrant, the police recovered the mower and charged the man who had it with theft, or more precisely, conversion.

The section about wild animals in captivity is interesting because it has been wrongly argued that anyone who catches a wild animal and puts it in a cage does not own it. This argument incorrectly asserts that since the animal was born wild, the man who caught it only has it temporarily, and should it escape it is again free for anyone to catch and keep. If this were true, should a valuable circus animal escape, the finder could claim "finders keepers". The Code specifically states that the person holding the wild animal in a cage is the owner. However, it should be remembered that the laws against cruelty to animals still apply.

294. Except where otherwise prescribed by law, every one who commits theft is guilty of an indictable offence and is liable

(a) to imprisonment for ten years where the property stolen is a testamentary instrument or where the value of what is stolen exceeds two hundred dollars, or

(b) to imprisonment for two years where the value of what is stolen does not exceed two hundred dollars.

Special circumstances surrounding the taking of cars have called for a special section that separates taking cars for fun from stealing cars for profit. Since the intent of some persons is really to borrow the car without lawful authority, but not to keep it, charging them with theft is not realistic. For just such occurrences, the next section was adopted:

295. Every one who, without the consent of the owner, takes a motor vehicle with intent to drive or use it or cause it to be driven or used is guilty of an offence punishable on summary conviction.

POINTS TO PONDER

1. What would be wrong if an employee of a clothing store wears articles of clothing that belong to her employer and then returns them?

2. If a shopper took an item off the shelf and put it in his pocket how can the store prove that he did not intend to pay for it when he got to the cashier?

3. According to some studies, stealing has become so widespread that everyone is doing it, and many people now believe there are different degrees of honesty, i.e., it's all right to steal from strangers but not your friends, or it's all right to steal from your employer because he doesn't pay you enough, or it's all right to steal from big companies or from the government because they're so big it can't hurt them. Are there different kinds of honesty?

4. Does the law support the saying, "finders keepers"?

Trespass

The Lord's Prayer contains a passage, "Forgive us our trespasses as we forgive those who trespass against us." Christian teaching refers to trespasses as all sins against us, but court records would show that we are not as willing to forgive trespass in our narrower definition as the church would have us do.

Property rights and protection of property form a constant theme running through our laws. We resent those who infringe, poach, invade, squat, encroach, or even mooch a little on our property. We often assume they have other motives, such as theft.

The Criminal Code states that everyone in possession of movable property has a right to prevent a trespasser from taking it from him, as long as bodily harm is not done to the trespasser. If the trespasser persists in laying hands on the property and in trying to take it from the rightful possessor, then the trespasser commits assault and may be arrested.

Regarding real property, the Criminal Code goes further:

40. Every one who is in peaceable possession of a dwelling house, and every one lawfully assisting him or acting under his authority, is justified in using as much force as is necessary to prevent any person from forcibly breaking into or forcibly entering the dwelling house without lawful authority.

41. (1) Every one who is in peaceable possession of a dwelling house or real property and every one lawfully assisting him or acting under his authority is justified in using force to prevent any person from trespassing on the dwelling house or real property, or to remove a trespasser therefrom, if he uses no more force than is necessary.

(2) A trespasser who resists an attempt by a person who is in peaceable possession of a dwelling house or real property or a person lawfully assisting him or acting under his authority to prevent his entry or to remove him shall be deemed to commit an assault without justification or provocation.

147

A man observed several snowmobilers on his property. He went out and informed them they were on private property and ordered them to leave. They refused. The man took hold of one snowmobiler and began pulling him towards the public road. The snowmobiler hit the man. The snowmobiler was convicted of assault. His defence that the property owner had no right to lay hands on him was rejected. The court affirmed that the property owner had a legal right to use reasonable force to remove a trespasser. The snowmobiler had no legal right to strike the property owner. By resisting violently, the trespasser commits assault.

It is important to be sure whose property you are on. Should a dispute arise, do not seek a confrontation which might lead to violence. Rather, wait until you can ascertain the property ownership through court records. Trespassing remains an unpopular offence—few property owners appreciate it.

The "prowler" is another character who is not popular around town. Whatever his motive—peeping, stealing, or just walking around at night, he is resented and feared. Anyone who comes onto private property at night, without a valid reason, is immediately suspect.

173. Every one who, without lawful excuse, the proof of which lies upon him, loiters or prowls at night upon the property of another person near a dwelling house situated on that property is guilty of an offence punishable on summary conviction.

Police answered a complaint about a prowler and found a man standing beside a house. At the police station, he contended that he was "just looking for a place to relieve myself." His explanation was not deemed adequate and he was fined upon summary conviction.

POINTS TO PONDER

1. If a person refuses to leave your house when ordered to do so, may you throw him out bodily?

2. If your property (movable) goes onto someone else's real property, may you trespass to retrieve it? For example, you hit a ball onto another person's property. May you go onto that property to retrieve it?

Civil Rights and Individual Safeguards

In our western society, the rights of the individual are protected from encroachment from either other citizens or government. Thomas Jefferson in the American Declaration of Independence said that "We all are endowed by our Creator with certain inalienable rights." By "inalienable" he meant that these rights may not be taken away. Often governments come under criticism for "coddling criminals" when they grant suspected persons these rights. But without them, government would have unlimited powers and the individual none.

Some of the important aspects of civil rights with regard to arrest and trial for criminal offences are explained in this section. The entire text of the Canadian Bill of Rights is also included as an appendix to this book.

ARREST

The power of arrest is given to peace officers by the Criminal Code. In fact, if a police officer *fails* to arrest someone where required, he may himself be guilty of an offence.

There is a correct way for a policeman to make an arrest:

He must tell you that you are under arrest—*if you ask.*
He must tell you the charge—*if you ask.*

For example, if a policeman says something like "You had better come down to the station with me," and you go along willingly, you cannot later claim that you were unlawfully arrested. If you ask, "Am I under arrest?" and he refuses to answer or says, "No," then you are free to go on your way. If he says, "Yes," then you may ask what the charge is. If you do not ask, you cannot claim later that he did not tell you the charge. If you ask, and he refuses to answer, there is no lawful arrest.

(This case is not a real one, but has only been made up to illustrate lawful arrest. It is doubtful that any peace officer would be so unaware of what constitutes lawful arrest.)

A man is found in a parking lot near the scene of a burglary. A policeman suspects he was connected to that offence.

Officer: You had better come with me.
Man: Why?
Officer: Just get in the police car.
Man: Why should I?
Officer: You'll find out when we get downtown.
Man: Am I under arrest?
Officer: Don't get cute, buddy! Just get in the car.

At this point, there is no lawful arrest.

Man: Am I under arrest?
Officer: Yes.
Man: What is the charge?
Officer: I'll tell you that after I talk with the desk sergeant.
Man: I want to know now.

At this point, there is no lawful arrest.

Officer: The charge is breaking and entering.

At this point, the arrest is lawful.

If you feel you are being unlawfully arrested, you may resist. However, there is a danger in doing this. If you are wrong and the arrest is lawful, you can be charged with resisting arrest and assaulting the peace officer. It is far better to comply at the time and argue the question of unlawful arrest later. Obtain the name of the policeman, and if possible of any witnesses to the arrest. *You may sue a policeman for unlawful arrest.* At the time of the arrest, object verbally but not offensively. This means, inform the officer that in your opinion the arrest is unlawful. Do not use foul language or insult him. When you reach the station, repeat to the desk officer that your arrest is unlawful. Repeat this to every officer or official who examines or questions you. However, use no forcible resistance, for if the

151

arrest is later held to be lawful, your resistance will be another charge against you.

A group of young men were hanging around a shopping area. Some were clowning and a large glass window was smashed. Police attempted to arrest three of the young men. One denied he had anything to do with the matter and resisted arrest. He kicked one officer and bit the second. He was later found innocent on a charge of malicious damage to the window, but while his friends went free, he was held for resisting arrest and assaulting the two officers. For these charges he was convicted and heavily fined.

In Canada, there is no such thing as holding a person for questioning. Either you are under arrest or you are not.

A policeman may have a written warrant for arrest, but he does not need one in every circumstance. It would be senseless to require an officer to produce a warrant when he has just surprised two men robbing a bank. The Criminal Code provides for immediate arrest:

450. A peace officer may arrest without warrant

(a) a person who has committed an indictable offence or who, on reasonable and probable grounds, he believes had committed or is about to commit an indictable offence,

(b) a person whom he finds committing a criminal offence, or

(c) a person for whose arrest he has reasonable and probable grounds to believe that a warrant is in force within the territorial jurisdiction in which that person is found.

It is not really surprising that an officer may arrest anyone whom he finds actually committing a crime. More interesting, perhaps, is the wording of paragraph 450 (a) that says he can arrest anyone he believes is *about to commit an indictable offence.* The police are not required to sit back and wait until the offender actually commits an offence. For example, if police are watching a bank for robbers, and the robbers appear outside, the police may grab them immediately. They do not have to wait until the robbers go inside and rob the bank.

An interesting case was *Regina v. Beaudette (1957)* in which the defendant was evicted by two officers from a bar for being noisy. When the defendant got outside, he entered into a conversation with another man, and the other man said, "Drive me home." The defendant started walking towards the parking lot with the other man. The same two officers, having overheard this conversation, arrested the defendant. The grounds for the arrest were that the defendant was highly intoxicated, and that he was intending to drive a motor vehicle. In other words, the officers believed he was about to commit an indictable offence and arrested him before he could do it. The defendant claimed that there was no justification for the arrest and that he was not told the reason for his arrest. The court held that under the circumstances, the officers were justified in their belief that an offence was about to be committed.

Every citizen has a legal obligation to assist a policeman in making a lawful arrest, if the policeman asks. This does not mean you must endanger yourself, nor do you have to help collect evidence or investigate crimes.

A citizen may arrest anyone he actually catches committing an *indictable* offence or who he has reasonable grounds to believe has committed a criminal offence and is escaping from and freshly pursued by persons who have the lawful authority to arrest him. He must tell the person he is under arrest and turn him over to a police officer as soon as possible. Reasonable force may be used to make such an arrest.

A citizen found a burglar in his home and confronted him with a shotgun. He said, "Stand right there, you're under arrest." The police were called and the arrest was deemed lawful.

A citizen found a burglar in his home and shot and killed him on sight. This was neither lawful arrest or justifiable homicide since excessive, not reasonable, force was used.

A citizen was annoyed by a drunk who was making a lot of noise and singing obscene songs in the street in front of his house. He went out and arrested the man. This was not lawful arrest; the drunk was not committing an indictable offence.

Generally, a citizen should not attempt an arrest unless he believes immediate arrest is necessary, that the offence is serious, and that the police cannot arrive in time. The only instance in which the power of arrest for a summary conviction offence is given to a private citizen is when an offence is committed on or in relation to his property.

A peace officer may arrest without warrant for a summary offence where he actually finds the accused committing the offence. It is essential that the offence be committed in the officer's presence. If the person is innocent, and the alleged offence is only a summary offence, then the arrest is illegal, even if the officer had probable grounds to believe the person guilty. Even if the person is guilty, the arrest is illegal if the crime was not committed in the presence of the officer.

If a citizen requests an officer to arrest a person whom the citizen contends committed an offence, and the citizen will sign the complaint or charge sheet, then the officer may make the arrest and the citizen must run the risk of false arrest and possible civil action arising from false arrest.

BAIL

If you have been arrested, you may not have to wait in jail until your trial. Often there is no reason to assume that an accused person will take flight or commit another offence while out awaiting trial.

A justice or magistrate may grant *bail* by requiring you to put up a sum of money or pledge property to guarantee that you will appear for your trial. Or, he may ask you to guarantee verbally that you will appear and release you on your own recognizance. If you fail to show up for trial, the bail is forfeited and a bench warrant is issued for your arrest.

In Canada, there are no professional bondsmen. These are men who make a business of lending people money to pay their bail and charging them interest for the loan. This practice is illegal in Canada, although it is common in the United States. Here, bail money may not be borrowed, but a friend or relative may assist you in raising bail.

154

You don't have an automatic right to bail. It is granted only to persons with relatively good records and to those who have not committed serious offences. Public safety demands that some offenders be held in jail until their trial. However, a magistrate cannot refuse to grant bail unreasonably, nor can he set it so high that it cannot possibly be paid. Your lawyer can appeal a refusal to grant bail.

Recently, a Bail Reform Act has been passed. Under its provisions it is possible for a person to be released without seeing a magistrate. Police officers can serve a summons to appear in court rather than make the arrest and take the person to a police station. The summons, much like a traffic ticket, lists the charge and informs the person that if he doesn't appear, a bench warrant will be issued. If the officer is not sure, he can arrest the person and take him to the station. The desk sergeant, after identifying the person and ascertaining that he is an established resident, may release him on his own recognizance, giving him a summons to appear later in court. This permits responsible persons to be summoned to court without detention in jail, fingerprinting, etc. The significance is in the attitude. Traditionally, it was held that an accused person had to convince authorities that he should be permitted out on bail. He had to show good reason why he should not be kept in prison until his trial. Now, the attitude is that authorities must show good reason why he should be kept in prison until his trial.

CONFESSION

An admission of guilt may be made by an accused person at any time in the proceedings against him. Naturally, such admissions or confessions are appreciated by the Crown since it then no longer has to prove its case.

Should one or should one not make an admission? What purpose is served by doing so? Often the accused feels great guilt and a strong urge to "confess and get it over with". Or he may hope for lighter punishment in return for his cooperation. He may believe there is so much evidence against him, that denial is useless. Whatever the reason, confessions are frequently obtained by authorities. What are the techniques used by professional police interrogators?

The "Tough guy, soft guy" Method

Copied from German army intelligence, this approach requires two interrogators. The first man is tough. He comes on hard—threatens personally to crucify the accused. He'll make sure he gets the maximum penalty. He tells the accused that the police have all the evidence they need to send him away for ever. He offers no comforts, not a cigarette nor a drink of water. He goes away supposedly to wrap the case up.

Now, the soft guy takes over. He has been listening to the tough guy and he doesn't approve of the way he has been treating the accused. He's sympathetic—offers the accused a cigarette and maybe a cup of coffee. He understands—and urges the accused to relax and listen to reason. He'd like to help him get off easy. A confession would solve everything. Otherwise, the tough guy will be back again. The accused relents and confesses to his "friend", the soft guy.

The "We know you did it" Method

This uses the approach that the interrogator already has complete proof of the crime. He refuses to discuss guilt or innocence—as far as he's concerned that's established; he just wants to know why. He keeps repeating lines such as "We know you did it—all we need are a few details. Why pretend any longer?" He suggests possible escape pleas for the defendant: "Joe, why did you kill that guy? Did you have a fight? My guess is that he was looking for you. Maybe it was self-defence. You're the only one who can clear this thing up." The tactic here is to try and get the accused to elaborate on what the police supposedly know already; that he is guilty.

The "Blame someone else" Method

If several persons are involved in one offence, they are questioned separately. The interrogator encourages each to blame the other, hoping that way to fill in the details. One interrogator may enter a room and say to an accused, "You may as

156

well quit stalling—your pal just confessed." Or, he may enter and say, "Your pal confessed. He says you killed that guy." At this point, the unwary accused blurts out a denial and tells how the other person actually committed the crime. The maxim: Divide and conquer.

Are these methods illegal? Do they violate the rights of the accused? Can the confessions be used in court? In most instances, confessions obtained this way are perfectly admissible. The requirements of a valid confession are:

The confession must be given freely, without physical or mental coercion to induce fear.

The accused must not be offered favourable treatment or lessened punishment by a person in authority.

The accused must know his statement may be used against him.

The confession must be a self-incriminating one only—not an accusation casting the blame on someone else. Such a statement is not a confession at all, but rather an accusation that must still be proven.

Note that a confession is not invalid simply because the accused did not first see a lawyer. The police do not have an obligation to ask the accused if he wants a lawyer—the accused must ask the police for permission to contact one. If the accused cannot find one, he should ask to see the Legal Aid Duty Counsel before court the next morning. Until he sees a lawyer, the accused should say nothing about the alleged offence and sign no statements or submit to any tests, except the breathalyzer test.

A confession unlawfully obtained may be refuted any time. One lawfully obtained cannot be refuted.

Canadian rules of evidence do not allow a confession to be read in court in which the accused blames someone else. Such a statement is not a true confession at all.

Two men were arrested for illegal possession of narcotics. One confessed, the other did not. They were tried together. The

Crown attempted to introduce the confession of the one man, but the defence objected. The court permitted only parts of the confession to be read—the parts in which the confessor discussed his own part in the crime. Other parts, relating to the role his friend played were ruled inadmissible.

If the two men were tried separately, the confession could be read at the trial of the confessor, but not at the trial of the other man. Nor could it be considered evidence. However, if the Crown could get the confessor to testify directly against his friend at his trial, that would be acceptable.

An accused person should give serious thought before making any statements to the police. Unless he has a valid reason to give evidence voluntarily, it is far better to remain silent and let the Crown establish its case in court.

SOME EVIDENCE RULES

The question as to what evidence may be used against an accused is covered by the Canada Evidence Act and by other cases which are used as precedents. It is a vast subject, and cannot be dealt with in complete detail. For our purposes, we shall only consider some of the more interesting evidence rules. However, it should be pointed out that if a witness wishes to seek the protection of the Canada Evidence Act, he must be very careful and very precise.

Husband/Wife Relationship
Generally, a husband cannot be compelled to disclose any communication made to him by his wife during their marriage; nor can the wife be compelled to disclose what her husband told her. This is not true all of the time. Certain offences, because of their nature, permit the Crown to call a husband or wife as witness against his or her spouse. Examples of such offences are sexual offences or crimes committed while the spouses are separated.

158

Incriminating Questions

Canada does not have a "Fifth Amendment" like the United States. A witness cannot refuse to answer a question on the grounds that it may tend to incriminate himself. However, the witness is protected in that the answer he gives shall not be used at any trial or civil proceeding against him. Although our law requires a witness to answer, it does afford him protection by guaranteeing that what he says cannot later be used to convict him.

Handwriting

Evidence rules permit handwriting experts to testify as to the genuineness of handwriting. Both sides may introduce such evidence.

Evidence of Child

A child who does not understand the nature of an oath may be permitted to testify without an oath. No case may be decided upon the unsworn testimony of a child alone. It must be corroborated by some other material evidence.

Best Evidence

Generally, the best evidence rule insists that in every circumstance, the best means of introducing the evidence must be employed. If the original document is available, a photocopy should not be introduced. If a person can personally testify, he must do so. A statement from the person can only be introduced if he is unable to testify. For example, a laboratory report was ruled inadmissible when it became apparent that the laboratory technician who prepared the report was available to testify. A medical report is not acceptable if the doctor can testify.

Circumstantial Evidence

There are generally two kinds of evidence, direct and circumstantial evidence. Direct evidence can be subject only to one error—human mistake. If Jones saw Smith shoot Brown, this is direct evidence. It is, of course, possible that Jones suffers from poor vision and did not see Smith shoot Brown, but made a

159

mistake and just thought he did. However, if Jones found Brown dead and Smith standing over him with a gun, he cannot say Smith shot Brown. The circumstances indicate that he might have shot him, but there is no direct evidence that he did. Smith might have found Brown shot with the gun beside him and picked it up.

Circumstantial evidence requires persons to draw a conclusion or inference from the evidence. A conviction upon circumstantial evidence alone is dangerous, but not impossible. If the jury is satisfied that the circumstantial evidence is overwhelming, a conviction is possible.

Inflammatory Evidence

The judge will not allow evidence to be introduced solely for the purpose of inflaming the jury's anger against the defendant. In the famous Truscott trial, the judge refused to permit the prosecutor to admit into evidence photographs of the murder victim, because the photographs did not contain any evidence which could not be presented by the oral testimony of witnesses. The judge ruled that photographs of the victim would only be ghastly representations which would anger the jurors and prejudice them against the accused. If the photographs contained some clue which could not have been introduced through any other method, the judge might have admitted them into evidence.

HABEAS CORPUS

A writ of *habeas corpus* is directed to the person having custody of another person, demanding that he "have the body" (*habeas corpus*) in court.

The *Habeas Corpus* Act was passed in England in 1679. At the time, it was fairly common practice to arrest an inconvenient person, throw him into a dungeon, and leave him there for life, without ever having a trial. If he died, his body might be disposed of and the family might never know what had become of him. The *Habeas Corpus* Act permits any interested person to petition the court to bring the arrested person to court and:

Explain the nature of the charge against him and by whom the charge was brought, and

Proceed with a trial without undue delay.

Habeas corpus is a vital part of our law. If a trial takes a long time in coming, the Crown must show that it is proceeding as quickly as possible. In some places there are so many criminal cases pending that an accused may wait in jail a year or more for his trial date. This is not considered undue delay, since the Crown is not deliberately delaying cases, this waiting period is true of all cases.

JUVENILE DELINQUENTS

A juvenile delinquent is an offender under the age of sixteen. He may not be locked up with adults or brought before a magistrate, but is referred to juvenile court, where supervision is stressed rather than punishment. This is not true in every case, since criminal action can be brought against someone as young as the seven-to-fourteen age bracket as was discussed earlier. This is rare, however. In juvenile court proceedings, words such as "conviction" and "sentence" are not used. Trials are held in private, and outside parties may not attend. The names of juveniles may not appear in newspapers. A child awaiting trial is kept in a detention home rather than a jail.

Children do not have to testify under oath since they may not understand the meaning of the oath anyway. After examining the case, if he finds the child to be "delinquent", the judge may take one of several actions:

Release the child to the custody of parents on his promise of good behaviour.

Release the child under the supervision of a probation officer.

Place the child in an industrial home if he is over the age of twelve.

Place the child in a foster home.

If a fine or damages are awarded, the judge may order the child to pay if he has means. He may order the parents to pay if the parents have contributed to the commission of the offence by neglecting to exercise due care of the child. This does not mean parents are automatically responsible for every wrong act a juvenile commits. Sometimes the child is clearly out of control of his parents and the court must exercise control.

If it is necessary to detain a juvenile, he must be kept separate from adult prisoners. No juvenile may be kept in a jail or police station where adults are imprisoned. As soon as a suspect is identified as a juvenile, he must be turned over to juvenile authorities. Even if a juvenile is to be tried in criminal court, he must not be jailed with adult offenders, but kept apart.

Adults who contribute to the delinquency of a child can be fined $500 or imprisoned for two years or both. "Contributing" means any act which aids, abets, or encourages a child to become a juvenile delinquent. This includes his parents.

A fourteen-year-old boy was in trouble with the law several times. His probation officer reported to the judge that an older male friend was providing the boy with alcohol, urging him to skip school, and generally influencing him to commit increased numbers of offences. He told the boy he didn't have to report to his probation officer if he didn't want to. The judge summonsed the friend and ordered him to cease all contact with the younger boy. When the man failed to comply, the judge sentenced him to six months imprisonment.

Recently the government introduced the Young Offenders Act to replace the Juvenile Delinquents Act. This took a harder line towards young law-breakers. It was not passed by Parliament, and critics called it too harsh. Supporters of the Act claimed it would have dealt effectively with chronic trouble-makers whom the juvenile courts seem powerless to handle. Whether the Young Offenders Act will be reintroduced is undecided at the moment.

LEGAL AID—RIGHT TO COUNSEL

There is nothing in the Criminal Code which guarantees everyone a lawyer. The Criminal Code does not prohibit conviction because a lawyer is not present at the trial. However, the law and court procedure have grown so complex that it is known that it is very difficult for an accused to understand the proceedings against him. In 1966 the Legal Aid Act was passed. The ideal of this Act is to insure that no one is convicted just because he cannot raise enough money to provide a defence.

Does this mean that everyone gets a good lawyer, free? It does not mean that. Legal aid is afforded only to those who otherwise could not afford it. The basis, then, for extending assistance is financial need.

In Ontario, the procedure is as follows. An application is made to an Area Director of the Legal Aid Plan. This application is given to the Department of Social and Family Services for investigation into family income, debts, etc. The Department advises the Legal Aid Director how much, if anything, the applicant can pay for his own legal costs. If legal aid is authorized, the applicant pays the plan the part of the cost that is assigned to him.

The applicant may then choose his own lawyer, as long as the lawyer is a member of the Law Society of Upper Canada. The applicant presents a certificate to the lawyer stating the amount the Legal Aid Plan will pay him for representing the client. Neither the court nor the general public knows how much the client is paying and how much the Plan is.

It is possible to get legal aid for civil cases and criminal cases. The only prohibitions against extending aid are cases of

Defamation—injuring a person's reputation

Breach of promise of marriage—failure to go through with a promised marriage

Alienation of affection—causing a husband or wife to lose the affection of his or her spouse by attracting the spouse away

Loss of female service through seduction or rape—causing the head of a household to lose the work of a female in his house

Proceedings due to an election—arguments over the outcome of an election

By January 1971, over 300,000 persons had received assistance in some form from the Legal Aid Plan. If you are arrested, ask to see the Duty Counsel as soon as possible. The Duty Counsel will assist you with the immediate matters such as preliminary hearing, bail, etc. He will get you started with your Legal Aid application so you can quickly obtain legal counsel of your own.

PROBATION

Probation is a condition which a judge may order rather than imprisonment. If criminals are to be urged not to repeat their offences, jail is often not the place to do it. If the offender is of previously good character, and the offence is not too severe, the judge may pass sentence then "suspend" the sentence. This means the accused does not have to serve the sentence, *if* he complies with the conditions of the probation. This may include any or all of the following:

Report to and be under the supervision of a probation officer.

Provide support for his family.

Abstain from alcohol.

Abstain from owning or carrying a weapon.

Make restitution for any damages caused.

Remain within the jurisdiction of the court. Notify the court of any change of occupation or address.

Make reasonable efforts to maintain employment.

Have no association with known criminals or bad companions.

Comply with any other conditions which the court may establish.

A time period is set on the probation and if the probationer fulfils his probation order, his sentence is terminated. If he violates the terms of his probation, the judge may recall him to court and order his original sentence served. Failure to report to the probation officer is often the reason for ordering the sentence served.

An interesting development in the United States has been to employ ordinary citizens as probation officers on a voluntary basis. Because probation officers already have too many cases, the need for additional help has led to forming Committees for Probation which perform the same function as the regular probation officers. From first reports, it is working very well since the man on probation feels he is dealing with an ordinary person, not a semi-policeman. Another method, used in Philadelphia, is to employ ex-convicts as probation officers. These men can often communicate well with offenders because they have been through the same sort of problems. They can speak from real experience when they urge their clients to follow the terms of their probation and avoid prison.

Probation is not perfect, but our prisons are too full already. Canada has a higher percentage of its male population in prison than the U.S. or any European country. Penologists are concerned that prisons are "crime schools" where criminal talents are exchanged. If first offenders can be kept out of this environment, society will benefit.

QUESTIONING

Most Canadians believe they have the right to tell the police nothing at all. This is not completely true. For example, the Ontario Highway Traffic Act requires a driver to show his driver's licence to a police officer. If he does not have his driver's licence, he must tell the officer his correct name and address. Failure to do so may lead to arrest.

If a policeman finds you wandering around, he may ask that you explain your purpose. You must give a logical explanation of what you are doing. Refusing to answer or giving a foolish answer may lead to arrest for vagrancy.

If you are arrested, provide the police with your correct name, address and age. After that, anything you say is up to you. You may answer all questions or say nothing, that is your choice.

SEARCH AND SEIZURE

The right of search is one that often leads to disagreements with the law. Different officials have different powers under different Acts.

For example, Canada Customs officials have extraordinary powers to search vehicles and persons entering Canada. Cars can be literally disassembled looking for contraband. Suitcases are gone through thoroughly, and items can be X-rayed for hidden compartments. The problem of drug trafficking has intensified customs searching and seizure. If contraband is found, the entire vehicle may be seized and later forfeited if conviction is obtained.

The policeman who stops you for speeding does not usually ask to see in your trunk. If he did, would you have to let him? He may only search your car if he believes that illegal liquor, drugs, or weapons are within it. If he finds any, he may seize the entire vehicle and contents. If the driver is convicted both illegal substances and automobile are forfeit. If the policeman arrests the driver, he may search the vehicle as a natural course of the arrest. However the police may not search cars at random without justification.

If the police want to search any building, including a home, they first require a search warrant from a justice. The justice must be satisfied that there are reasonable grounds that what they are searching for will be found inside the building before he may grant the search warrant. The police must carry out the search on the date shown on the search warrant, during the hours of daylight, unless the warrant states "at any time". The police may seize the items they were searching for, or any other illegal contraband found on the premises. If you refuse to admit police who have a search warrant, they are permitted to break in.

The RCMP sometimes employ a writ of assistance. This is a court order compelling the person to whom it is presented to render whatever assistance the police require of him. These writs are used chiefly in the search for drugs. It permits the holder to enter any place in Canada and compel the assistance of any person therein, without a search warrant.

166

A team of RCMP officers raided a store where drugs were believed hidden. They presented the store owner with a writ of assistance. He refused to open a locked cabinet when they asked him to do so. The police broke the cabinet open, but found nothing. No drugs were found anywhere in the store. The store owner was convicted, however, for failure to adhere to the writ of assistance and assist the officers in their search.

The writ of assistance gives a great deal of power to the police, and the Canadian Bar Association has recommended several times that the right to use these writs should be repealed.

When can a policeman search you personally? Anytime after he has arrested you.

Two men were arrested after a burglary. Both were lined up beside their car and "frisked". Their car was also searched. Both searches were lawful without search warrants since the two men were already under arrest.

A policeman can also search you without arresting you under one of two conditions: if he believes you are carrying a prohibited or restricted weapon, or if he believes you have illegal drugs on your person.

Drug search is a very general power given to police to deal with a very difficult problem. If drugs are believed inside a building, the police may enter without warrant. Your car can be searched as can your home. Anyone in the suspected premises can be searched, too. A known narcotic user or trafficker can be searched without warning. An interesting case was the following:

Rex v. Brezack (1949)
Two RCMP constables were waiting for a known narcotics peddlar. Information told them he was transporting illegal drugs in his mouth in waterproof capsules. When they saw him, they rushed him and knocked him down. One officer clamped his throat to prevent him from swallowing the evidence. The other officer put his hand in the man's mouth to search for the drug

capsules. The unhappy Mr. Brezack bit the officer's hand. No drugs were found in Mr. Brezack's mouth, but they were later found in his car. He was also charged with unlawfully resisting the search and assaulting the officer by biting him. Mr. Brezack's lawyer contended that lawful search did not extend to forcing your hand in a person's mouth and that the accused was perfectly justified in biting anyone who did so. The judge did not agree, retorting that since the circumstances were that the officers believed the drugs to be in the mouth, that it was their clear duty to search there.

If you believe a search is illegal, protest, but do not resist violently. Your resistance may turn out to be a bigger offence than what you are accused of, if you are wrong about the search being illegal. Your lawyer will be best equipped to argue the case in court if you do not forcibly resist, but object only verbally.

SELF-DEFENCE

When two cowpokes shot it out at high noon, the winner claimed he had killed in self-defence. After all, the other cowboy was trying to kill him! This kind of duel is illegal now and cannot be claimed as self-defence. Other forms of defence are also not acceptable.

Self-defence cannot exceed what is *reasonably necessary* under the circumstances, to protect your person, family, or property. Only if you are assaulted with violence, may you resist with violence. You may inflict bodily harm or death on your attacker when you believe he intended the same fate for you.

A man saw a prowler outside his window. He shot and killed him with a deer rifle. He held that this was self-defence. This claim was denied, since there was no evidence that the prowler intended bodily harm or death to the home owner.

You cannot claim self-defence if you provoke the assault yourself, then strike down the attacker.

A man arguing with another man kept saying, "C'mon, hit me. I dare you. You haven't got the guts." When the other man finally did attempt to hit him, he struck him more quickly and caused bodily harm. His claim of self-defence was rejected because he provoked the attack. Without the provocation, the attack would not have occurred.

The law may consider that self-defence would have been best afforded by running away. If it is obvious that the person claiming self-defence could have declined to fight, that he could have run away or retreated in some manner, then the claim is not valid. Only after an attempt is made to retreat or decline combat, and further escape or retreat is impossible, should a person engage in combat with his attacker. Refusal to avoid a fight because of personal pride or simply a desire to fight rules out a plea of self-defence. Defending your own "honour" or someone else's honour is not self-defence, either.

A soldier sitting in a night club with a woman became annoyed when another man at the next table kept trying to make conversation with her. The man then moved to the same table and sat next to the woman, trying to make conversation. The soldier ordered him to "get lost." The man retorted, "She doesn't seem to mind, why don't you get lost?" The soldier angrily stabbed the man through the heart. His claim of self-defence and protecting his female companion was not accepted, since there was no real threat to them of bodily harm.

Self-defence must be kept strictly within the meaning of the terms "reasonable force". Over-reacting or fighting, when running would suffice, will rule out a claim for self-defence and may lead to conviction of a serious crime.

POINTS TO PONDER

1. Do you think wiretapping should be totally disallowed as a violation of civil rights? Or should police be permitted to tap lines if they obtain a court order?

2. The right to legal counsel is an established one, but is afforded only according to financial need under the present legal aid plan. Should counsel be provided free in all cases? Should Canada adopt a "Public Defender" to handle all cases? Since the Crown initiates criminal action, should the Crown be required to pay all the costs?

3. The Attorney General of Quebec wants all citizens in Quebec to carry identification cards with their photograph and fingerprints. Do you think such cards constitute a threat to civil liberties?

4. The Canadian Bar Association recommended that Parliament abolish writs of assistance. Do you agree?

5. A citizen may arrest a person committing an indictable offence. Would you favour extending this to include summary offences as well?

Criminal Court Procedure

Having been arrested, the accused person has one basic question for his lawyer: "What is going to happen now?"

The procedure which the criminal court system in Canada follows is outlined in this next section.

If we assume the accused man is able to appear before a magistrate (in Ontario, called a provincial judge), his case will probably be "remanded" until a later date. This means that the Crown is not fully ready to begin proceedings against the accused. It is also understood the accused also needs time to prepare his case. Hopefully, bail will be granted and the accused will be free while he consults his lawyer.

EARLY PROCEEDINGS

When the accused is first ordered to appear by arrest or summons, the nature of the offence will be discussed. Serious offences are called "indictable offences" and less serious ones are called "summary offences". "Summary" means they can be dealt with rapidly and easily. Some offences are considered both indictable and summary, and the Crown may choose which procedure it wants to follow.

The magistrate must also place the offence into one of three categories:

Those over which the magistrate has absolute authority

Those over which the magistrate has authority with the consent of the accused

Those over which the magistrate has no authority

These offences are listed below in more detail.

Those over which a Magistrate Has Absolute Authority
Theft, value not exceeding $200
Obtaining money by false pretences, value not exceeding $200
Possession of stolen property, value not exceeding $200
Attempted theft
Obstructing a police officer
Keeping a gaming house
Selling lottery tickets
Cheating while playing a game
Keeping a bawdy-house
Driving a motor vehicle while licence is suspended
Common assault
Assaulting a police officer engaged in execution of his duties
Failure to collect prescribed tolls or fares

If the accused has been charged under one of these sections, the magistrate *must* hear the case. The accused cannot insist upon a trial by jury in a higher court, simply because the offence does not merit the time and expense of a major trial.

At the other end of the scale, we find offences so serious that the magistrate cannot hear them, they must be heard by a judge of the Supreme Court, with or without a jury. The magistrate cannot hear them even if he was willing to.

Offences over which a Magistrate Has no Authority
Treason
Alarming her Majesty
Intimidation of Parliament or a legislature
Inciting to Mutiny
Sedition
Piracy
Piratical Acts
Bribery of a public official
Rape
Criminal negligence
Capital murder
Manslaughter
Threatening death or injury to another person
Accessory after the fact of treason or murder

172

Taking a bribe by a judicial officer
Attempting any of the previous offences
Conspiring to commit any of the previous offences

For the remainder of the indictable offences, the accused may elect to be tried in one of three ways, by a magistrate, by a County Court judge without jury, or by a County Court judge with jury (possibly a Supreme Court judge).

The following words are put to the accused:

> You have the option to elect to be tried by a magistrate without a jury; or you may elect to be tried by a judge without a jury; or you may elect to be tried by a court composed of a judge and jury. How do you elect to be tried?

PRELIMINARY HEARING

If the accused elects trial by judge or trial by judge and jury, the magistrate will hold a *preliminary hearing* to decide whether there is sufficient evidence to justify committal for trial. He will hear brief statements from witnesses and determine if the case which the Crown has thus far put together warrants continuing against the accused. If he believes not, he may dismiss the charge. If he believes there is sufficient evidence to justify trial, he will either confine the accused or free him temporarily on bail.

If we summarize in chart form what has transpired so far, it will appear as shown on the next page.

TRIAL BY JURY?

At this point, it might be well to reflect upon the wisdom of choosing a trial by jury. The nature and character of juries are fascinating, and many books have been written about them. Defence lawyers spend a great deal of time studying the psychology of juries. The accused should not automatically choose trial by jury assuming that his chances of getting off are greater. There are advantages and disadvantages to jury trial.

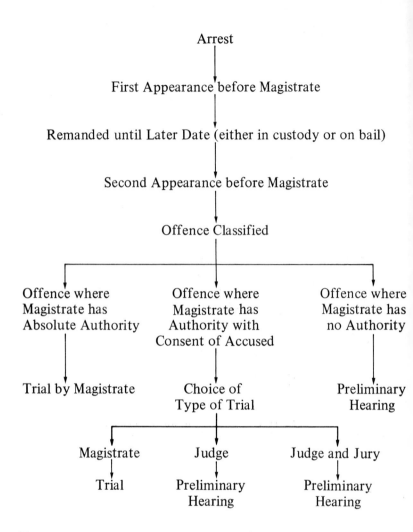

To use an example, a man arrested for breaking and entering might follow this course:

Arrest ⟶ First Appearance (bail denied) ⟶ Remanded in Custody ⟶ Second Appearance ⟶ Offence Classified as one where Magistrate Has Authority with Consent of Accused ⟶ Accused Chooses Trial by County Court Judge ⟶ Magistrate Holds Preliminary Hearing

What Advantages?

The verdict in criminal cases must be unanimous. If the defence can convince one juror, conviction is barred.

Jurors may represent the same social level as the accused, which may be lower than that of a judge. Jurors may have more empathy with the accused than a judge.

The right to challenge jurors should provide for an unbiased jury.

A good defence lawyer knows how to work on juries. His rhetorical abilities will make a greater impression on jurors than on a judge.

What Disadvantages?

Jurors can be very prejudiced against certain defendants: they can be influenced by the social level, appearance, race, nationality, etc. of the accused. A jury might take one look at a hippie-type accused of drug possession and be convinced of his guilt before any evidence has been presented.

Jurors can be swayed by a good Crown attorney. Just as a defence lawyer can work on a jury, if the prosecutor is good, he will be equally successful.

Jurors often don't understand the law and may reach a wrong verdict simply because of a misunderstanding, despite what the judge instructs them to do.

Rather than demand trial by jury automatically, the accused should discuss the advantages and disadvantages with his lawyer before deciding how to be tried.

PLEA BARGAINING

Prior to the actual trial, an "unofficial" process called plea bargaining takes place. Because the cost and time of a trial, particularly a jury trial, is very great, a "bargain" can sometimes be reached between the defence counsel and the Crown attorney.

The defence counsel has a fair idea of how much evidence is stacked against his client. He knows the odds in favour of obtaining a complete acquittal if the Crown pursues its case to get a guilty verdict on the major offence. The defence counsel visits the Crown attorney in his office and discusses the case, particularly with regard to the chances of the accused being found not guilty. The bargain which the defence counsel seeks is that if the Crown will not insist upon a conviction for a major offence, the defendant will plead guilty to a minor offence, or to a lesser included offence. For example, if the Crown will drop the charge of burglary, the defendant will plead guilty to possession of burglary tools. Or, if the Crown will not press for conviction of criminal negligence with a motor vehicle, the defendant will plead guilty to dangerous driving.

With plea bargaining many cases can be settled quickly and without costly trial. The accused receives some punishment, but not the maximum. The Crown is assured of a conviction for some offence, even though it is not the maximum offence. The Crown is trading conviction and sentence for a serious offence for conviction of a lesser offence, but is at least assured conviction. If the Crown refuses to bargain, then it is possible that the defence will succeed in a complete not guilty decision. The defence attorney cannot of course engage in plea bargaining, without the consent of the accused. No defence attorney should urge a plea of guilty for his client when the accused insists upon his innocence.

If the Crown attorney is sure of conviction of the major offence, it is unlikely that he will do any bargaining, since he is under no pressure to do so.

GRAND JURY

In certain provinces, before a case can go to jury trial, it must first be examined by a grand jury. The procedure is for the Crown to prefer what is referred to at this stage as a bill of indictment before the grand jury. The hearing by the grand jury is held in secret and only Crown evidence and witnesses are presented. The accused and the defence counsel are not allowed to be present during the hearing. After hearing the Crown evidence, the grand jury must decide whether there is sufficient evidence to warrant trial by petit jury. If so, they declare a "true bill" and the bill of indictment is now verified as an indictment. If not, they declare "no bill" and the case will not be brought to trial. In instructing the grand jury, the judge may use words similar to the following:

> If, on all the evidence and the law as explained to you, a petit jury of reasonable men would not convict, even if no answer was given, you should find no bill. If, on all the evidence and the law explained to you, there is sufficient reason to believe an offence has been committed and that it was committed by the accused, then you should find true bill.

A grand jury originally consisted of twenty-three persons, but was gradually reduced until in Ontario it presently consists of seven persons. A simple majority of four may reach a verdict. England abolished the grand jury in 1933. In Canada, grand juries were abolished in Manitoba in 1923, in British Columbia and Quebec in 1932, and in New Brunswick in 1959. Alberta, Saskatchewan, the Northwest Territories never had grand juries. The system still exists only in Ontario, Newfoundland, Nova Scotia and Prince Edward Island.

Critics argue that the grand jury is a waste of time and money. They also add that having a secret hearing without allowing the accused to be present, does not fit into our modern legal philosophy.

Grand juries can also be called together for special purposes, such as inspecting jails or other institutions maintained by public money, and to investigate reports that persons are held in jail without trial because of undue delay in trial preparation.

SELECTING THE PETIT (PETTY) JURY

To serve on a petty jury, a person must be a Canadian citizen, have not been convicted of an offence for which he served over twelve months in prison, and must not be employed as a lawyer, law student, clergyman, policeman, and sometimes doctor or teacher. Some other groups are also excluded. The prospective jurors are summoned to court where each name, address, and a number is placed on a card. Then, the process of empanelling the jury begins.

The defence attorney and the Crown attorney may challenge

177

"for cause" any prospective juror because he (a) is prejudiced, (b) has strong personal feelings about a certain type of offence, (c) has prior knowledge in the case, (d) is related to the accused, or (e) has already made up his mind about the guilt or innocence of the accused. There is no limit as to how many jurors may be challenged for cause. For example, Melvin Belli, who defended Jack Ruby over the shooting of Lee Harvey Oswald, the alleged murderer of President John F. Kennedy, challenged for cause every prospective juror who had seen the shooting on television. It just so happened that Ruby shot Oswald right in front of the cameras and nearly every person in the United States saw it. It took many months to find a jury of persons who had not thus been witnesses to the shooting.

In addition to challenging jurors for cause, jurors may be removed by "peremptory challenge" by the defence. A peremptory challenge has no cause, it is just a right given to the defence to remove from a jury a person whom it believes will be difficult and unsympathetic. The number of such challenges varies with the offence:

For an offence for which the possible penalty is death—twenty challenges

For an offence for which the possible penalty is five years or more in prison—twelve challenges

For all other offences—four challenges

The Crown attorney also has four peremptory challenges and may also direct up to forty-eight jurors to "stand by" until other jurors have been examined. A juror who stands by is not eliminated. He only goes to the end of the line again until it is seen if twelve jurors can be found from among the other prospects. If a full jury is not formed, those who stood by are called again until the jury is filled.

THE TRIAL

The events in a trial are fascinating, and a full description would not be possible since they vary with every offence. The sequence of events follows this general arrangement:

Opening arguments by the Crown attorney. He will stress how he will establish guilt.

Opening arguments by the defence attorney. He will stress what the Crown must prove, and how they will fail and he will try to establish either innocence of the accused or that there is insufficient evidence for conviction.

Evidence and witnesses presented by the Crown.

Cross-examination of the Crown's witnesses by the defence attorney. (Cross-examination takes place as each witness is called, not all at once at the end.)

Evidence and witnesses presented by the defence attorney.

Cross-examination of defence witnesses by the Crown.

Closing arguments by the Crown attorney. He will stress how the evidence leads to an inescapable verdict of guilty.

Closing arguments by the defence attorney. He will again stress the lack of evidence against the accused and the evidence supporting a verdict of not guilty.

There are many legal principles which apply during the trial. The judge is the final authority in determining whether evidence is admissible and whether a witness may answer a certain question. If there is doubt, the judge will have the jury leave, then hear the evidence himself. If it is admissible, the jury returns to hear it. If not, the jury will never hear it.

The accused does not have to testify. If he wants to do so, he must be prepared to undergo cross-examination by the Crown attorney.

No one may mention that the accused has been arrested or convicted before. However, if the defendant chooses to testify, he may be asked if he has ever been convicted of a criminal offence as a "test of his credibility".

A complete transcript is kept of the entire trial. Items introduced as "exhibits" are kept in the court's possession until the end of the trial after which a description or photograph is made of them. Some exhibits are the property of others and some are so large the court could not keep them. The record of trial may be very important in later appeals.

During cross-examination, each side may ask leading questions rather than just direct questions. Leading questions suggest the answer sought. They are very powerful when posed by a master, and here lies the danger of allowing the accused to testify. A defence attorney knows that his client may "break" under relentless cross-examination and may keep him off the stand. He may also not call certain witnesses because they will be unable to stand up to cross-examination. Our criminal court is truly an adversary system with each side determined to destroy the other's case. While this may be difficult on the individuals concerned, it is hoped that the ruthlessness may also bring out the truth.

INSTRUCTING THE JURY

After the closing arguments, the judge must instruct the jury as to its duty. Since jurors may not understand the law, and have not been allowed to read the Criminal Code during the trial, they often can't distinguish between fine points of law, such as the difference between murder and manslaughter. The judge must carefully explain the law as it applies to the case. He will advise them on what they must base their decision and how to go about it. This is a very important part of the proceedings, for if the judge instructs the jury wrongly, the jury will reach a wrong verdict. Famous appeals have stemmed from the manner and wording which the judge put to the jury during his instructions. In the case of *Rex v. Woolmington*, (1935) the judge instructed the jury in this way:

> The Crown must satisfy you that this woman, Violet Woolmington, died at the prisoner's hands. They must satisfy you of that beyond any reasonable doubt. If they satisfy you of that, then he (the defence lawyer) has to show that there are circumstances to be found in the case which alleviate the crime so that it is only manslaughter, or which excuse homicide altogether, by showing that it was a pure accident.

The wording of this instruction was challenged in an appeal. The appeal contended that the judge wrongly instructed the jury by saying that the defence must prove that the slaying was manslaughter or accident. Rather, argued the defence attorney, the judge should have instructed the jury that the whole burden of proof must be on the Crown that the accused committed murder. The Crown must prove beyond all reasonable doubt that the killing was murder, not manslaughter or accident. By wrongly instructing the jury, the judge caused them to reach a wrongful verdict of guilty. The appeal was successful and the case was ordered to be tried again.

After the judge instructs the jury, they retire to the deliberation room. Then the judge will ask both the Crown attorney and the defence attorney if they have any complaints about the manner in which he instructed the jury. If they have valid objections, the judge may recall the jury and instruct them again.

THE VERDICT

A jury must reach a unanimous decision in its verdict of guilty or not guilty. Failure to reach a verdict will usually lead to the judge recalling the jurors and instructing them again in their duty. If no decision is reached, the jury is discharged. This is often referred to as a "hung jury", and the judge may order the entire trial repeated with a new jury. The jury may also find the accused not guilty of an offence, but guilty of a lesser included offence. For example, a charge of criminal negligence with a motor vehicle may be returned with a verdict of not guilty of criminal negligence, but guilty of the lesser included offence of dangerous driving. Many offences have lesser included offences within them.

Also, if a jury does not find the accused guilty of an offence, it may find him guilty of an *attempt* to commit that offence. For example, a charge of theft may result in a verdict of not guilty of theft, but guilty of attempted theft.

The verdict is announced by the foreman of the jury, who is a temporary spokesman elected by the other jurors. While they are deliberating, no one may speak to the jurors, not even the bailiff who is sworn to keep them sequestered (isolated) during the deliberation. If the jurors wish to see exhibits again, or hear

181

part of the transcript of the trial read again, they may send a request to the judge for the material. The judge will hear arguments from both counsellors before deciding to admit the material to the jury deliberation room.

Situations can arise where the judge must intervene somewhat in the process of the jury reaching a verdict.

It is a principle of law that the judge is the sole judge of the law, and the jury is the sole judge of the facts. In a thorough trial, the jury must determine the verdict based solely on the facts presented. This is the responsibility of the jury and the judge will not interfere. However, in other cases, it may be a matter of *law* that the accused must be found not guilty, and the judge will tell the jury that.

For example, suppose a woman is accused of killing her husband by poisoning. The evidence shows that they had a fight, and that after eating a lunch which the wife made, the husband died suddenly. However, no evidence is introduced to show that the cause of death was poison. No medical examination is introduced to show that poison was found in the dead man's system. At this point, the Crown closes its case. The defence attorney would immediately rise and move that the judge direct the jury to find the accused not guilty. The judge would probably agree, because he knows that a necessary element for the proof of murder is missing, and that without it, no jury could properly convict the accused. There is no sense going further with the trial, or having the defence call witnesses. As a matter of *law*, the evidence is simply insufficient to convict, and the judge will instruct the jury to find the accused not guilty.

This directed verdict of not guilty saves time and expense in the trial, and prevents a wrongful verdict of guilty being brought in, which the accused would later easily have reversed in an appeal.

SENTENCING

After the jury has reached its verdict, it has no further function. In some cases it may recommend mercy or leniency. If a verdict of guilty has been reached, the judge must next sentence the accused. He will probably delay sentencing to allow both sides to present arguments concerning the character and previous record of the convicted person. He will often also direct the probation office to compile a pre-sentence report about the person's family life, education, employment, and so forth. Having heard about the crime, the judge now wishes to know about the criminal.

What influences a judge as he decides upon the sentence? Studies show that judges rely on a combination of many factors, including:

The nature and circumstances of the offence
Previous convictions
Public sentiment and pressures concerning certain types of offences
The judge's own prejudices concerning certain types of offences
The character of the convicted person—public safety
The age of the convicted person

If several offences are committed and perhaps several "counts", or occurrences, are listed under each, the judge may award one sentence for all, separate sentences for each to run concurrently—at the same time, or separate sentences to run consecutively—one after the other. For example, a person convicted on two counts of assault causing bodily harm may be sentenced separately on each count. He then may be required to serve both sentences consecutively, increasing his jail time greatly.

APPEALS

The right to appeal is vital to our criminal system. Without it, wrong decisions would never be corrected. Appeal cases often bring out the most dramatic and important decisions in legal history.

Originally, appeals were made to the king. A person who felt a case was decidedly wrongly, or that the law was unjust, could appeal to the king to intervene personally on his behalf and decide the case himself on the basis of "equity". Equity means that the king decided the case on its own merits and disregarded previous decisions. Later, the king permitted equity to be administered by one of his officials, the Lord Chancellor. Now, equity is an inherent function of our courts of appeal.

An appeal must be made within thirty days of conviction. During this time, the convicted person is kept in a provincial jail, rather than being sent to a federal penitentiary.

The appeal must have valid grounds, not be made just to delay punishment. Appeals may be launched for one or more of the following reasons:

The judge erred by admitting evidence that should not have been admitted.
The judge wrongly instructed the jury.
The jury was not impartial.
The facts were not brought out.
New evidence is now available.
The law contravenes basic rights, or conflicts with other laws.

Interesting appeals have recently been made to the Supreme Court of Canada regarding the mandatory breath test for drivers. The first appeal was based upon the idea that the test violates the basic right not to incriminate oneself. The appeal was denied. Another appeal was based on the fact that when the bill was passed in Parliament, it contained a section that said the police must give the driver a sample of his own breath in a "suitable container". The purpose of this was to provide the accused with a sample of the evidence which would be used against him. He could then have it analyzed by a chemist elsewhere, and perhaps argue against the police claim that his test showed he was impaired. However, this section of the bill was not declared into force when the rest of it was. The Governor in Council only declared part of the law in force and deleted the part about "a suitable container". The reason it was deleted was that there was as yet no such thing as "a suitable container" for breath samples. The appeal argued that until the entire bill is declared in force, none of it can be enforced. The Supreme Court disagreed and the appeal was denied.

A successful appeal from a conviction will result either in the conviction being quashed, which means the accused will go free, or in an order for a new trial.

The Crown also has the right to appeal. If the accused is found not guilty, the Crown may appeal on questions of law alone, but not on questions of fact or mixed fact and law as the defence may. Such appeals, if successful, will result in a new trial.

Most appeals from Magistrate's Court go to County Court. All others go to the appeals division of the provincial Superior Court, which in Ontario is called the Ontario Supreme Court. From there, appeals go to the Supreme Court of Canada. The system is complex, and there is no need to memorize it in detail. The appeal system is shown graphically on the next page.

A GOOD SYSTEM?

While the steps taken in reaching a verdict in a criminal case may seem complex, they nonetheless form the best system in existence today—or at least Canadians think so. No other system gives so careful attention to ensuring the verdict is right, that the rights of the accused as well as those of society are represented, and that if errors are made a method of correcting them is available. No one should, in the words of Justice Oliver Wendell Holmes, "have anything to fear from the bench."

THE CORONER'S JURY

Before we leave the subject of court procedure, a special explanation should be added here regarding the coroner's inquest. No one is exactly certain when the office of coroner first began, but records as far back as the twelfth century mention coroners.

The coroner is a medical officer whose basic duty is to inquire into the deaths of all persons within his territory, usually a county. Every one knowing that a death has occurred must notify a coroner. With this notification a medical-legal inquiry begins. The coroner has the power to take possession of the body and to make such investigations as are necessary to determine the cause of death. If the death occurred from

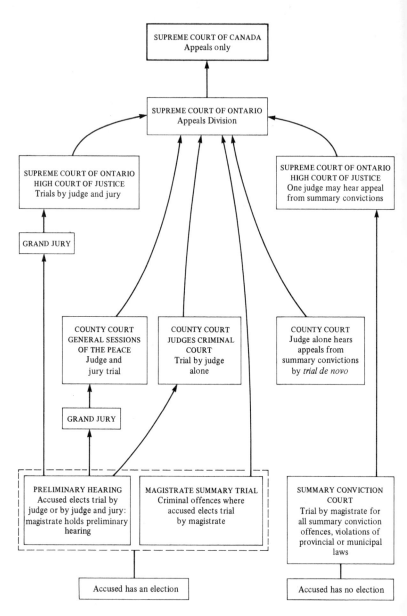

In Ontario, a Magistrate = a Provincial Judge

natural causes, the doctor in charge will issue a death certificate and no further investigation will be held. In other cases the coroner may decide to hold an inquest. In Ontario the inquest will involve the coroner and five jurors chosen by him from the voting list. It will examine evidence and hear witnesses to determine, when, where, how and by what means the person met his death. An inquest is nearly always held where the death may have been due to violence, negligence, misconduct, malpractice, a disease or sickness not treated by a doctor, misadventure or dangerous practices, or where it occurred under suspicious circumstances during pregnancy.

The coroner's inquest is run by the coroner, sometimes with the help of a Crown attorney. Persons appearing at an inquest are entitled to legal counsel to examine or cross-examine on their behalf. A person facing criminal charges involving a death can refuse to testify. Witnesses are advised of their rights under the Canada Evidence Act.

The duty of the coroner's jury is to reach conclusive findings that can lead to changes in the law. The jury is not to fix blame of death upon any person or draw conclusions on points of law. The jury can make recommendations as to how similar fatalities can be prevented. A simple majority of the jurors can reach a verdict.

The verdict of the coroner's jury is not binding on the community at large. If the jury recommends that safety devices be installed on a certain machine, no one has to follow that recommendation. The jury cannot make law, only recommendations in the field of law.

A coroner's jury inquiring into the death of Mary Lou Markland, twelve, of RR 8, Picton, Ontario on August 25, 1971 in an accident involving a pickup truck, ruled her death accidental. The jury recommended that no passengers be permitted to ride in the back of pickup trucks unless they have a box-covered back; that the Department of Transport insist on more stringent eye examination for drivers, and that highway shoulders be paved more on curves. Mary Lou was thrown from the rear of the truck, driven by her mother, when the vehicle overturned. Mrs. Markland had good sight in only one eye. The coroner was Dr. C.R. Richmond, the Crown attorney, Richard Sheely.

Despite these recommendations it is doubtful that the Department of Highways rushed out and paved the road shoulders, nor did they suddenly cause the Department of Transport to change its eye test.

What value does the coroner's jury have in our legal system? Its chief purpose is to insure that deaths caused by violent or suspicious causes do not go undetected. Since a coroner is a medical practitioner, he can understand medical reports such as autopsies and explain to the Crown attorney why he feels an offence may or may not have occurred. The coroner's jury can propose useful ways to prevent fatalities, particularly from accidents.

Criticism of the coroner's inquest system has traditionally centered around the fact that inquests can have tremendous importance in subsequent criminal cases, but do not follow the rules of evidence of the courts or permit persons suspected of wrongdoing to remain silent. Ontario's revised system in 1973 eliminated many of the abuses that had existed in the coroner's inquest, but these improvements are not uniformly in force in other provinces.

POINTS TO PONDER

1. Some provinces have done away with the grand jury as unnecessary. Should all provinces eliminate it?

2. Plea bargaining is an unofficial action. Do you think it upholds or violates the principles of justice?

3. Jury trials are longer and more expensive. Would you favour reducing the number of jurors from twelve to six, or eliminating jury trial except for very serious offences?

4. Some countries do not permit cross-examination of witnesses unless the judge believes false testimony has been given. Would this be a good practice for Canada to adopt?

5. The United States is seeking to introduce a federal law which would prohibit convicts from filing appeals once they have entered a penitentiary. All appeals would have to be made final before entering the penitentiary. Do you think this discriminates against convicted persons, or would it be a good law for Canada to adopt?

Canada's Federal Prisons

Few people see the inside of a federal penitentiary. The exceptions are those who are imprisoned there and those who work there. Tours as such are not permitted. In order for a writer to have access to a prison, he must get the permission of the Solicitor General of Canada.

I put together the material here on the subject of prisons after such a visit and interviews with various officials of the penitentiary service.

WHO GOES TO A PENITENTIARY?

Not every lawbreaker ends up in a federal penitentiary. A person convicted and sentenced to two or more years in prison will serve that sentence in a federal penitentiary. A shorter sentence than that will be served in a provincial jail. The penitentiary system itself is divided into three different kinds of prisons: maximum security, medium security, and minimum security. The chief deciding factors on where a man will serve his sentence are the danger which he would represent to the public if he escaped, and whether or not he will attempt to escape. A convict is placed in a penitentiary on the following basis:

Maximum Security
The convict is expected to make active attempts to escape, and if he did escape, would be dangerous to the public.

Medium Security
The convict is not expected to make active attempts to escape, but if given the opportunity to escape, would probably do so. If he did escape, he would probably not be dangerous to the public.

190

Minimum Security

The convict is not expected to make any attempt to escape, and if he did, would not be dangerous to the public.

RECEPTION

When a convicted person is taken to a penitentiary, he first goes to a reception center. Here he is issued all the items which he will need in prison, including three prison uniforms, eating utensils, toilet articles, etc. More importantly, he is examined by a classification board. This board is made up of the warden, a psychiatrist, a sociologist, a criminologist, a minister or priest, and the chief training officer. His offence and attitude and desire to improve himself are considered. He undergoes psychological tests and numerous interviews. His background, often taken from case histories prepared by social agencies, is studied. Every attempt is made right from the beginning to insure the man has a worthwhile chance of rehabilitation. The prison rules and regulations are explained to him, and he is often placed in the care of an older trustworthy convict to help him adjust to the routine.

THE DAILY SCHEDULE

The schedule will vary a lot from one institution to another, but in the medium security prison I visited, this is the schedule followed. The inmates rise at 7:00 a.m. They shave and wash in their cells, then take their eating utensils to the mess hall. If there is an eating area, they eat there. If not, they take their trays back to their cells. The morning work or study period is from 8:00 until 11:00. Each inmate knows where he is supposed to report, and goes there unescorted. Each shop or classroom instructor counts those present, and if an inmate does not show up, this is reported and a search is made. If he has absented himself without reason, he will be punished. The inmates work under the supervision of an instructor, not a guard. Guards are present only at exits, but are on call by phone from each shop. If an inmate refuses to work or causes a disturbance in his shop, a guard is called to come and take him back to his cell. He will be later punished by the inmates board. The inmates work at woodwork, machine, electrical and other skills. A prison is a total community, so they also perform the maintenance, cleaning, etc. Lunch is from 11:00 until 12:30. Again, each inmate moves about on his own. He reports back to his shop or class at 12:30 when the attendance is again checked. Work ceases at 5:00 p.m. and the evening meal is served. From 6:00 until 10:00 the inmate may do much as he pleases. There is a gymnasium and recreation room; he may watch television, play cards, go to the library, or just read or write letters in his cell. At 10:30 all inmates return to their cells for attendance and the cells are locked.

PUNISHMENT OR REHABILITATION?

There is considerable disagreement as to just why the convict is in the prison. Is he there to be punished, or to be rehabilitated? The central theme has been to put men in prison to prevent them from repeating their crimes. Prisons do not go very far back in our history. Traditionally, punishments were more direct, such as execution or mutilation by cutting off an ear or hand. The idea of imprisoning persons is fairly new. Originally, they were so incarcerated just to punish them. The idea was that this way they would be locked up for life and would suffer longer. However, when shorter prison sentences became common, the question of rehabilitation was brought to the fore. If these persons were to be returned to society, should not an attempt be made to improve their behaviour before letting them go? Now, most of those imprisoned are eventually released. The purpose of rehabilitation is to improve their attitude and approach to life by finding out what caused them to commit their offences and dealing with this cause. Then, when they are released it is hoped they will not repeat their previous behaviour. There is one great difficulty in this idea, generally called the prison dilemma. If a man has not been able to function in a free society, and is put in prison, how can the prison teach him the way to behave in a free society when the prison itself is anything *but* free? Rehabilitation takes the form of trying to educate and train the man in order to improve his ability to support himself so that he does not turn to crime for economic reasons. At the same time, psychological studies are made, and the individual is asked to try to understand why and how his former behaviour was unacceptable. No one claims present efforts at rehabilitation are a complete success but an attempt must be made.

THE INCORRIGIBLES

There are no uniform statistics about prisoners that are very enlightening to anyone. It appears on the surface that about 40 to 50% of those released from prisons will commit another offence and return. These incorrigibles constitute about 80% of those arrested. What we have is a build-up in prisons of the same persons who repeat offences and return again and again. First offenders make up only about 20% of the population of the prison. This problem of building up a group of professional prison dwellers is world wide. There seems to be no answer to it, but one theory being tried is that posed by Dr. Maxwell Jones, a British penologist. Dr. Jones contends that repeaters are so institutionalized that they only function well inside the prison. Once allowed to leave, they immediately get into trouble because they do not know how to function outside at all. The answer which Dr. Jones suggests is to force responsibilities and decision-making on inmates while in the prison. Make them run things. Make them serve on committees which take decisions. Consult them about prison problems. Unless they are required to exercise some sort of leadership and independence, they will remain institutionalized and will never be able to leave the prison with any degree of confidence in themselves.

The evidence indicates that some inmates are habitual criminals. They cannot be allowed freedom under any circumstances because all efforts at rehabilitation have failed. They spend most of their time in prison discussing crime with other inmates and actively planning their next crime.

There are criminals who are so dangerous that it would be

unthinkable to allow them to prey on society. These men are usually doomed for life to a maximum security prison, a very undesirable fate.

Some inmates are convinced that society has never given them a chance and will start hounding them again as soon as they are released. There are those who cannot stay out of trouble due to alcohol or bad companions. Whatever the reason, it appears that about 40% will remain incorrigible, and hope really rests with the other 60%.

PRIVILEGES

All mail, in and out, is subject to censorship, although it is not all read. No one has the time to read all that mail. All incoming mail is opened before being given to the inmate, because it is possible to mail small amounts of drugs or even weapons inside an envelope. An inmate may send a sealed letter to his M.P.P., M.P., or the Solicitor General. Inmates must buy their own writing materials and stamps.

All inmates have visiting privileges, unless they are being punished for something. There is no limit to the number of visits, although they may be curtailed if they are interrupting the inmate's work or study times. The prison tries to take special consideration for visitors who have travelled long distances to see an inmate.

The visiting is not always done through the barred window. This method is normally used only for maximum security inmates who cannot be trusted. The present system in the prison I visited involves a large, open room where inmates can sit and talk with visitors on couches and chairs. The security is upheld by "skin frisking" the inmate before and after the visit. He enters a small room, takes off every item of clothing, then is thoroughly searched by a guard, including "recesses" such as mouth, ears, rectum, etc. This tight security pays off. During the visit, visitors may not hand anything to the inmate. To insure this, all visiting rooms are under the eye of a guard watching through a glass panel.

THE PECKING ORDER

A definite social system exists among the inmates within a prison. Some are held in high esteem and others are despised. The order seems to depend largely upon the offence the person committed on the outside. Highest in the order are daring offences such as single-handed robberies. Lowest are "dirty" crimes such as sex offences, child beating or molesting, etc. The drug addict does not fit very well into the pecking order and is somewhere off to the side. Prisoners often prey violently upon those whom they regard as deviates. During the 1971 Kingston riot, it seems reasonably clear that the inmates who were killed were attacked because of the nature of the offences they had committed on the outside. There are groups or gangs which develop in the prison, with natural leaders coming to the front. The prison officials know who these leaders are, and they seldom have trouble with them because the leaders do not want trouble. They are running a smooth organization inside the prison, they have no desire to rock the boat and get the prison authorities on their back. There is little evidence that the groups fight each other.

DISCIPLINE

If an inmate breaks a rule or misbehaves in any way, the prison must discipline him. Some prisons have an inmates board, which may be comprised of the warden, the deputy warden in charge of custody, and the deputy warden in charge of staff training. They hear complaints against inmates from guards or instructors. A mild offence may mean a warning. A serious offence may mean loss of privileges and a written report in their file. Too many such reports will hurt their chance of early parole. The warden may put the inmate into "disassociation", which means he is placed in a separate cell area where he cannot mingle with the others. During this period, he also gets reduced rations. For three days, all meals are mush and bread and water. The rest of the time, he gets his meals without any extras such as dessert or gravy. He may be given corporal punishment, or whipping. This is administered with a leather strap on the buttocks, and can go up to fifteen strokes. It is very painful, and seldom used today. If the inmate continues to be a problem, he may be moved to a maximum security prison, where life is much less comfortable. He also runs the risk of having to serve his full sentence. Every inmate has what is called statutory remission of his sentence when he enters the prison. This means that if he behaves well, one-fourth of his sentence will be remitted or removed. For violations of rules, the warden can take away thirty days of that remission. The regional director of penitentiaries can take away ninety days of that remission. The Solicitor General can take it all away.

ESCAPES AND RIOTS

Two problems which plague prison officials are escapes and riots. Escapes are seldom made from within the prison, although this is not impossible as inmates have demonstrated. The old-fashioned bars have been replaced in many prisons with a new item, a single window with concrete-covered steel bars running through it that defies sawing.

Most escapes take place from outside the prison. Sometimes prisoners who are out on temporary absence passes do not return. This is termed an escape. Many inmates are allowed to leave the prisons every day to go to work or college. They return each evening, and except for a few people, no one in the outside world knows who they are. Other inmates work on the prison farm outside the walls, to produce fresh vegetables for the prison. Those who are allowed outside the prison are seldom dangerous if they escape. Others have escaped while being transported. One jumped from a window of a moving bus while being transported from one prison to another. He had entered the washroom while his guard waited outside, and managed to squeeze out. Others have escaped from hospitals after undergoing medical care.

Riots are another major problem, although there are not as many riots as the press might like us to think. Riots usually stem from poor conditions inside the prison. Poor food, for example, may spark a riot, but food in most Canadian prisons is rather good. Ontario penitentiary kitchens draw the same food as the Canadian Army. (Of course, members of the Armed Forces may argue that this is hardly a blessing.) Riots are usually started by a few persons. Then others get caught up in the excitement and the riot is on. The best way of dealing with a riot is to move in quickly before the inmates get organized and arm themselves with crude weapons. However, the prison staff may not have enough men to move in without calling reinforcements, so there may be a delay. If there is a delay and the riot gets into full swing, it is usually better to negotiate with the rioters than attack them since bloodshed will probably result. The guards inside the prison do not carry guns, since the inmates might get the guns away from them and be much more dangerous.

SUICIDE

Suicide in prison gets a lot of publicity, although there are fewer suicides per capita inside prison than outside. This is not a major prison problem. Most suicides occur at the beginning of the sentence, when the inmate is at his lowest ebb psychologically, and may be unwilling or unable to face up to the long term ahead.

TEMPORARY ABSENCES

As part of the attempt to rehabilitate them, inmates are sometimes allowed to leave the prison without guards for a short period, such as a weekend. They are trusted to return on time. This program worries some people, because on occasion the inmate does not return. This is deemed to be an escape. However, there is much to be said for this program.

There are about 7,000 persons in federal penitentiaries now. Many can be released without endangering public safety. If they are to merge successfully back into society, it is wise to let them do it a little at a time, rather than just to open the doors and say, "Go." The inmate has nothing to gain and everything to lose by failing to return. He faces loss of his statutory remission. He may be transferred from a minimum to a medium security prison. He will not get another leave.

197

The inmates themselves get very concerned when someone escapes while on a temporary absence, especially if the escape is well publicized as in the case of Yves Geoffroy. Geoffroy was serving a sentence for the murder of his wife and was allowed out of prison at Christmas 1971 to marry and, "provide a mother for his children." At the end of his leave he failed to return. He was finally captured with his new wife ten weeks later in Barcelona. Other inmates were extremely bitter because they felt that Geoffroy was "ruining it for the others," and that the whole temporary absence program was at stake, as newspapers published letters to the editor condemning the policy and Members of Parliament demanded full-scale investigations into the incident and the way the entire program was being carried out.

The absence policy involves risks, but as the Solicitor General, Jean-Pierre Goyer pointed out, the alternative involves more danger—the danger of not rehabilitating the man. For some inmates, nothing makes any real difference except ways of making life in prison a little easier. For many others, reforms such as the temporary absence program may well make the difference between successful rehabilitation and becoming an incorrigible.

PAROLE

Parole is an important part of Canada's penal system. An inmate may apply to the National Parole Board in Ottawa after serving one-third of his sentence. Parole is strictly selective and only about one-third of those who apply are granted it.

In his application, the inmate should state why he thinks he deserves to be placed on parole and should give details of his proposed parole program and plans for the future. Anyone may apply for parole on behalf of the inmate, or help him by arranging a parole program and community support.

Members of the staff at the inmate's prison are asked for reports on his attitude and progress, and these reports are sent to the Board's regional representative who interviews the applicant and gives an assessment of his suitability as a parole risk.

Ail this material is analysed at the Board's headquarters and a decision is made before the parole eligibility date.

The Parole Board takes the following factors into consideration when making its decision:

The nature and gravity of the offence.

Past behaviour.

Total personality of the inmate—whether he can be trusted in society.

Whether the parolee would be likely to return to crime and the possible effect on society if he did so.

The efforts made by the inmate during his imprisonment to improve himself through better habits, education and vocational training and how well they demonstrate his desire to become a good citizen.

Whether there is anyone in society who would help the inmate on parole.

The inmate's plans and whether they will aid in his rehabilitation.

What employment the inmate has arranged, or may be able to arrange.

How well the inmate understands his problem.

The acid test is whether the inmate has changed his attitude towards crime.

An inmate is on parole for the unexpired balance of his sentence plus any time he may have as earned remission. This keeps him under supervision for slightly longer than he would have been had he remained in jail. The parolee is subject to much the same sort of conditions as a person to whom the court has awarded a suspended sentence and has placed on probation.

Inmates and prison officials alike are often puzzled as to why one inmate is granted parole and anorther refused it. What does an inmate have to do, apart from just "being good"? It often seems difficult to understand just how the factors listed above relate to the actual decision. Then too, there is an outcry from the general public each time a person on parole commits a crime—the Parole Board is supposed to take the protection of the public into consideration; what is it about, endangering public safety by releasing dangerous criminals? The decision is often a hard one and mistakes are made. However, parole is obviously a good system for some convicts, and it would be inhumane as well as foolish to cancel the entire program because of a few failures.

The success or failure of parole depends greatly upon the public attitude. Many parolees who might have had a successful parole did not because of difficulties they encountered upon release. This problem is known to the Parole Board, hence the concern that a parolee have someone on the outside to work with him. Consider for a moment what happens. A man or woman is imprisoned for a period of years, perhaps ten or more. The outside world has changed dramatically, and among other things the inmate has forgotten how to deal with people other than guards and inmates. Suddenly the door is opened and he is thrust out with a strict warning not to get into trouble again. Possibly he knows no one in his former home town, or those he did know don't want to associate with an ex-con. Jobs are difficult to get with his record, and the only people who seem to care about him are other former inmates. He drifts quickly into bad company and his next offence is soon in coming.

Consider the opposite a moment. When he is released, someone is willing to act as a constant buddy to help the parolee readjust to the world he has been locked away from. If nothing else, at least he has someone to talk to! A job is available where the employer knows about his criminal record and is willing to accept the fact and believes he is getting a good worker who wants a chance. He is not shunned by those who knew him before he went to prison. He feels he has a real chance.

The success or failure, then, seems to have less to do with the man and more to do with the community. The parole officer tries to act as a friend, but he is often overworked and suspected by the parolee since he is also the man he must report to. Organizations like the John Howard Society or Elizabeth

Fry Society perform excellent work in the field of trying to help parolees get started and stay straight. At the same time, various communities have had good results with ordinary citizens working with parolees who have just been released, sometimes taking them into their homes for a while to help them adjust. (A young man honestly may not know what to say to a woman after not talking to one for ten years.) He has to be brought back slowly to the realities of life he missed while locked away. Failure to recognize the importance of the first few weeks on the outside, and neglecting the needs of the parolee, cause more parole failures than improper decision-making on the inside by the Parole Board. Despite cases such as the parolee who held up the taxi driver who picked him up at the gate, the Parole Board is usually right in selecting whom they release—it is the community that lets both the parolee and the Parole Board down by rejecting the man instantly. Parole does work; it can work better.

POINTS TO PONDER

1. Do creature comforts such as recreation, television, make prisons too comfortable?

2. Do you agree with the theory of Dr. Maxwell Jones that inmates should have greater participation in the running of prisons?

3. Should an inmate be punished for trying to escape, or should this be recognized as natural behaviour for a person in prison?

4. Canada has more persons in prison than England or the United States, calculated on a per capita basis. Can you think of any reasons why?

5. What would your concept of a model prison be?

Appendix: The Canadian Bill of Rights

When the delegates to the conference called to draw up the United States Constitution prepared the final document, they were very concerned with things such as the balance of power, the preservation of states' rights, the limitation of the authoritarian power of the various parts of the government, and they clearly spelt out the duties each part of government was to have. Representation was a major matter of debate, since small states were afraid the large states would overpower them if representation were based on population alone. The compromise was the creation of two houses, one based on population and the other, the Senate, based on equal representation, two per state.

With their work finished, the delegates began a new debate about civil liberties. The government was carefully designed, but what would limit the control of the government over the individual? Many of the delegates had come from Europe because of sad experiences where governments tyrannized and oppressed people on account of their political beliefs, religion, race, etc. Americans had waged revolution against Britain to combat what they considered oppressive government. Was the new Constitution to have no safeguards for the individual, protecting him from an oppressive government?

The delegates had read and were influenced by men such as Locke and Rousseau, who wrote about the rights of man—all men. They wanted something in the Constitution that contained guarantees of these rights. The result was the first ten amendments to the Constitution, later referred to as the Bill of Rights. These amendments contained guarantees against any government control over fundamental rights as speech, assembly, press, religion, and liberty.

Canada did not separate from England by revolution. Through the efforts of men who envisioned the possibility of independence within the British Empire, Canada came into official existence on July 1, 1867, when the Parliament of Britain passed the British North America Act, giving independence to Canada.

The British North America Act created the Canadian Parliament, the Provincial Legislatures, and the Canadian court system. It gave to each level of government powers to regulate and pass legislation. Final authority to Canadian laws was to be sought from the Governor General who was appointed by the monarch. The BNA Act continues to be the "Constitution" of Canada. It contains no Bill of Rights. Why not?

The failure of the British Parliament to establish a Bill of Rights when it drew up the BNA Act is not surprising. It did not occur to the lawmakers in England that government was naturally oppressive or that citizens need protection from government. Rather, the British regarded government as the protector of the people. Britain had no such thing as a Bill of Rights, so why would Canada need one?

For nearly a century, Canada did not follow the lead of the United States in drawing up such a list of guarantees of basic rights. It was generally felt that Canadians, because of their own history and the traditions of freedom and independence inherited from Britain, had no need of a formal declaration of rights that were already theirs. During the late 1950s, however, the increase in such things as demonstrations and protests—and the arrests that followed—caused some people to wonder what the future might hold. Canada cast a curious eye towards the United States and found that the one thing that was legally impenetrable in that country was the Bill of Rights. A move to have such a Bill in Canada gained momentum. As Prime Minister, John Diefenbaker fought a long battle to have the Canadian Bill of Rights finally approved by Parliament in 1959. Enacted in 1960, the Canadian Bill of Rights has withstood several difficult tests, but suffered something of a setback during the 1970 FLQ crisis in Quebec. As the reader will see, the War Measures Act has priority over the Bill of Rights in certain situations.

THE CANADIAN BILL OF RIGHTS

An Act for the Recognition and Protection of Human Rights and Fundamental Freedoms.

The Parliament of Canada, affirming that the Canadian Nation is founded upon principles that acknowledge the supremacy of God, the dignity and worth of the human person and the position of the family in a society of free men and free institutions;

Affirming also that men and institutions remain free only when freedom is founded upon respect for moral and spiritual values and the rule of law;

And being desirous of enshrining these principles and the human rights and fundamental freedoms derived from them, in a Bill of Rights which shall reflect the respect of Parliament for its constitutional authority and which shall ensure the protection of these rights and freedoms in Canada;

THEREFORE, Her Majesty, by and with the advice and consent of the Senate and House of Commons of Canada, enacts as follows:

PART 1

BILL OF RIGHTS

1. It is hereby recognized and declared that in Canada there have existed and shall continue to exist without discrimination by reason of race, national origin, colour, religion or sex, the following human rights and fundamental freedoms, namely,

(a) the right of the individual to life, liberty, security of the person and enjoyment of property, and the right not to be deprived thereof except by due process of law;

(b) the right of the individual to equality before the law and the protection of the law;

(c) freedom of religion;

(d) freedom of speech;

(e) freedom of assembly and association; and

(f) freedom of the press.

2. Every law of Canada shall, unless it is expressly declared by an Act of the Parliament of Canada that it shall operate notwithstanding the *Canadian Bill of Rights,* be so construed and applied as not to abrogate, abridge or infringe or to authorize the abrogation, abridgment or infringement of any of the rights of freedoms herein recognized and declared, and in particular, no law of Canada shall be construed or applied so as to

(a) authorize or effect the arbitrary detention, imprisonment or exile of any person;

(b) impose or authorize the imposition of cruel and unusual treatment or punishment;

(c) deprive a person who has been arrested or detained

(i) of the right to be informed promptly of the reason for his arrest or detention,

(ii) of the right to retain and instruct counsel without delay, or

(iii) of the remedy by way of *habeas corpus* for the determination of the validity of his detention and for his release if the detention is not lawful;

(d) authorize a court, tribunal, commission, board or other authority to compel a person to give evidence if he is denied counsel, protection against self crimination or other constitutional safeguards;

(e) deprive a person of the right to a fair hearing in accordance with the principles of fundamental justice for the determination of his rights and obligations;

(f) deprive a person charged with a criminal offence of the right to be presumed innocent until proved guilty according to law in a fair and public hearing by an independent and impartial tribunal, or of the right to reasonable bail without just cause; or

(g) deprive a person of the right to the assistance of an interpreter in any proceedings in which he is involved or in which he is a party or a witness, before a court, commission, board or other tribunal, if he does not understand or speak the language in which such proceedings are conducted.

3. The Minister of Justice shall, in accordance with such regulations as may be prescribed by the Governor in Council, examine every proposed regulation submitted in draft form to the Clerk of the Privy Council pursuant to the *Regulations Act* and every Bill introduced in or presented to the House of Commons, in order to ascertain whether any of the provisions thereof are inconsistent with the purposes and provisions of this Part and he shall report any such inconsistency to the House of Commons at the first convenient opportunity.

4. The provisions of this Part shall be known as the *Canadian Bill of Rights.*

PART II

5. (1) Nothing in Part I shall be construed to abrogate or abridge any human right or fundamental freedom not enumerated therein that may have existed in Canada at the commencement of this Act.

(2) The expression "law of Canada" in Part I means an Act of the Parliament of Canada enacted before or after the coming into force of this Act, any order, rule or regulation thereunder, and any law in force in Canada or in any part of Canada at the commencement of this Act that is subject to be repealed, abolished or altered by the Parliament of Canada.

(3) The provisions of Part I shall be construed as extending only to matters coming within the legislative authority of the Parliament of Canada.

6. Section 6 of the *War Measures Act* is repealed and the following substituted therefor:

"6. (1) Sections 3, 4 and 5 shall come into force only upon the issue of a proclamation of the Governor in Council declaring that war, invasion or insurrection, real or apprehended, exists.

(2) A proclamation declaring that war, invasion or insurrection, real or apprehended, exists shall be laid before Parliament forthwith after its issue, or, if Parliament is then not sitting, within the first fifteen days next thereafter that Parliament is sitting.

(3) Where a proclamation has been laid before Parliament pursuant to subsection (2), a notice of motion in either House signed by ten members thereof and made in accordance with the rules of the House within ten days of the day the proclamation was laid before Parliament, praying that the proclamation be revoked, shall be debated in that House at the first convenient opportunity within the four sitting days next after the day the motion in that House was made.

(4) If both Houses of Parliament resolve that the proclamation be revoked, it shall cease to have effect, and sections 3, 4 and 5 shall cease to be in force until those sections are again brought into force by a further proclamation but without prejudice to the previous operation of those sections or anything duly done or suffered thereunder or any offence committed or any penalty or forfeiture or punishment incurred.

(5) Any act or thing done or authorized or any order or regulation made under the authority of this Act, shall be deemed not to be an abrogation, abridgment or infringement of any right or freedom recognized by the *Canadian Bill of Rights*."

The Canadian Bill of Rights has been criticized for two hings which critics feel are lacking: The fact that the Bill of

Rights applies only to Bills passed by the Parliament of Canada, but not to those passed by the Provincial Legislatures, nor to any legislation that specifically excludes it. The War Measures Act can set aside the safeguards which the Bill of Rights upholds. The War Measures Act is a very drastic one, allowing arrest and detention without charge of persons accused of sedition, or attempting to overthrow the government. During the FLQ crisis, arrests numbered in the hundreds and some persons spent months in jail without charges against them.

Minister of Justice John Turner commented once that he would like a Bill of Rights that was supreme above all else and could not be set aside by the War Measures Act or any similar act. He added that to have a Bill of Rights which the government can set aside is little better than no Bill of Rights at all.

Possibly the unhappy side effects of the FLQ situation may bring about the drafting and passing of a new Bill of Rights, to be given a place of standing above all else.

POINTS TO PONDER

1. Would you favour a new Bill of Rights which cannot be suspended for any reason?

2. Should the Bill of Rights apply to laws passed by Provincial Legislatures as well as the Canadian Parliament?

3. What do you consider "inalienable rights"?

4. If the Bill of Rights were removed, would it cause real hardships for Canadians?

5. Should the Bill of Rights contain another safeguard— "freedom of political convictions"?

Test Yourself

The following are excerpts from criminal cases. In each case, establish the criminal law in question, the important facts that would help decide the case, and the probable outcome.

1. A fifteen-year-old girl ran away from a training school where she had been sent by a family court judge. She was found in Toronto living with a man who was having sexual relations with her. What possible offences could this man be convicted of?

2. A labour union found a tape recorder planted in their meeting hall. They realized that their plans were being related to their employer by whoever planted the machine, so they waited and grabbed two men who came to obtain the tape.

3. A man approached an eleven-year-old boy and offered him a dollar if he would accompany the man into an alley. The boy refused. Upon arrest, it was determined that the man was a known sex-offender.

4. A man published a book containing the names and telephone numbers of prostitutes. He was to receive payment from each prostitute who obtained a customer by means of this directory.

5. An elderly woman died from malnutrition. She lived with her daughter. The daughter admittedly neglected to look after her mother, but argued that she was not legally compelled to care for her in the first place.

6. A man, while intoxicated, sexually assaulted a woman whom he believed at the time to be his wife, but who in fact was not.

7. A man struck his wife and caused her serious injury. He had no motive for striking her. Medical examination showed that he had a cerebral tumour and was liable to outbursts of impulsive and motiveless action for which he had no explanation.

8. Two robbers entered a store and attempted a hold-up. The store owner had a gun under the counter and fired at the robbers. He missed the robbers but killed a customer. Who is responsible for the homicide—the store owner or the robbers?

9. Two men had a fight, and one received a serious knife wound. The wounded man did not realize how dangerous the wound was and only bandaged the wound. He did not seek help from a doctor or the hospital. Later, he lapsed into a coma and died. Is the man who stabbed him responsible for his death?

10. A man who needed money, faked a burglary and claimed that valuable items had been stolen. Before he could make a false claim to the insurance company, the police found where he had hidden the items which he claimed were stolen. He was charged with fraud. Would this charge lead to conviction?

11. A man drove his car through a stop sign and killed a pedestrian. He was in a total daze when police found him. Medical examination showed that he suffered from a form of epilepsy. He knew about this, since his doctor had discovered the disease more than a year before. Despite his doctor's warnings about blackouts, he continued to drive his car. Would he be responsible for the death of the pedestrian?

12. A man was a known sleepwalker. While walking in his sleep once, he was accosted by a constable who asked him why he was walking the street at night improperly clothed. When the constable got no reply from the man, he sought to arrest him. The man violently resisted. At his trial for indecent exposure and resisting arrest, the defence counsel argued that a sleepwalker should not be accosted, because in his sleep he cannot understand who is accosting him or why. The accused had thought he was merely defending himself. Do you agree?

13. A group of tenants were angry with their landlord over the poor condition of their residences which were very run-down. After the landlord refused to take any action towards repairs, the tenants marched into his office and threw a box of cockroaches all over the landlord. Would this constitute an offence?

14. Three men were adrift in a lifeboat. Because food and water were very low, two of the men threw the third, who was much weaker and sick from drinking salt water, overboard. They were charged with murder, but contended that what they did was necessary—otherwise all three would have perished. Are the two men guilty?

15. Police were trying to find out who in the city was receiving stolen goods from a gang of burglars. When they got a lead, they set a trap for the "fence" by selling him goods which they pretended were stolen, but in fact were not. The defence argued that since the goods were really not stolen, his client could not be convicted of receiving stolen articles. Do you agree?

16. Because school authorities were having trouble with alcohol and drugs, at a school dance they asked police to search all cars entering the school parking lot and everyone entering the door. Would the police have the power to conduct such searches?

17. A man was accused of committing a sexual assault against a nine-year-old girl. She testified without oath. There was no other evidence to substantiate her story. Would the man be convicted?

18. A man thought he saw someone prowling around his garage. He went outside carrying a pistol, which he had never registered. He found a prowler and arrested him, then called police. The police charged the homeowner with an offence as well. What would it be?

19. A man who had been smoking in bed fell asleep and started a fire. Two of his family died in the fire. What charge, if any, can be brought against him?

20. A convict, while escaping from prison, struck a guard on the head with a piece of steel pipe. The blow was not intended to be severe enough to cause serious injury, but only to render the guard unconscious for a while. The guard was hospitalized in serious condition, then developed pneumonia in the hospital and died. Is the convict guilty of the homicide?